A Philologist's Prayer

Robert St. Vincent Philippe

Our Teacher who art in English,
Proper be Thy Noun;
   Thy Adverb come,
   Thy Will (and Shall) be done
In Pronouns as in Interjections.

Give us this day our Passive Verb
And forgive us our Prepositions,
As we Decline those who Conjugate against us.

And lead us not into Conjunctions,
But deliver us from Adjectives,
   For Thine is the Comma,
   And the Period,
   And the Colon, forever.
                    Amen

THE BEST OF
Maledicta

**Edited by
Reinhold Aman**

RUNNING PRESS
Philadelphia, Pennsylvania

Copyright © 1977, 1978, 1980, 1981, 1983, 1984, 1985, 1987 by Reinhold Aman
Printed in the United States of America
All rights reserved under the Pan-American and International Copyright Conventions.

This book may not be reproduced in whole or in part in any form or by any means, electronic or mechanical, including photocopying, recording, or by any information storage and retrieval system now known or hereafter invented, without written permission from the publisher.

Canadian representatives: General Publishing Co., Ltd., 30 Lesmill Road, Don Mills, Ontario M3B 2T6. International representatives: Worldwide Media Services, Inc., 115 East Twenty-third Street, New York, New York 10010.

9 8 7 6 5 4 3 2
Digit on the right indicates the number of this printing.

Library of Congress Cataloging-in-Publication Data:
The Best of Maledicta.
1. Words, Obscene. 2. Invective.
I. Aman, Reinhold. II. Maledicta.
P409.M342   1987   080   86-31470

ISBN 0-89471-499-6 (paper)
ISBN 0-89471-500-3 (lib. bdg.)

Cover design by Toby Schmidt

This book may be ordered by mail from the publisher.
Please add $2.50 for postage and handling for each copy.
But try your bookstore first!
Running Press Book Publishers
125 South Twenty-second Street
Philadelphia, Pennsylvania 19103

MALEDICTA: The International Journal of Verbal Aggression, volumes 1–8 (1977–1985), is available from Maledicta Press, 331 South Greenfield Avenue, Waukesha, Wisconsin 53186.

Contents

FRONTISPIECE
1

INTRODUCTION
7

A WORD FOR IT!
by G. Legman
9

WINDY WORDS
A Glossary of Euphemisms for
The Expulsion of Intestinal Gas
by Bob Burton Brown
19

**HOW TO JUDGE PEOPLE BY
THEIR FARTING STYLES**
by L. Herrera
25

POONERISMS
by Richard Christopher
26

THE COCKNEY'S HORN BOOK
The Sexual Side of Rhyming Slang
by Leonard R. N. Ashley
29

IS FRENCH A SEXIST LANGUAGE?
Doing Cunteries in France
by Andrew R. Sisson
35

POTENTIATION OF A SPANISH INSULT
by Mario E. Teruggi
38

ITALIAN AND VENETIAN PROFANITY
by Giuliano Averna
40

ITALIAN BLASPHEMIES
by Giuliano Averna and Joseph Salemi
42

JAPANESE SEXUAL MALEDICTA
by John Solt
48

YUGOSLAVIA, HERE I COME
by Reinhold Aman
55

TEENAGE JOKESTERS AND RIDDLERS
A Profile in Parody
by Brigitta Geltrich-Ludgate
61

ACADEMIC GRAFFITI
by Weston La Barre
75

SIGMA EPSILON XI:
Sex in the Typical University Classroom
by Don L. F. Nilsen
77

DIALOGUE GRAFFITI
90

DISTURBING YOUR SEED
or, Greater Love Hath Onan
by Scott Beach
91

Contents

OFFENSIVE LANGUAGE VIA COMPUTER
by Reinhold Aman
93

POSTMATURE ORGASTRIX
by Reinhold Aman
94

LICENSE PLATE TABOOS
by Frank Nuessel
98

HOWARD UNIVERSITY LAW SCHOOL FINAL EXAM
103

THE JIMMY CARTER STATUE
107

TOM, DICK, AND HAIRY
Notes on Genital Pet Names
by Martha Cornog
108

RITUAL AND PERSONAL INSULTS IN STIGMATIZED SUBCULTURES
by Stephen O. Murray
118

A COMPILATION OF JOKES OFFENSIVE TO EVERYONE
141

VIET-SPEAK
by Dan Cragg
149

TAXONOMIC PORNITHOLOGY
Rules for the Naming of Egregious and Obscene Birds
by Douglas Lindsey
162

COMMON PATIENT-DIRECTED PEJORATIVES USED BY MEDICAL PERSONNEL
by C. J. Scheiner
170

NOT STICKS AND STONES, BUT NAMES
More Medical Pejoratives
by Lois Monteiro
174

SCRAM!
Or, 101 Ways to Sack Your Lover
by Laurence E. Seits and Robert M. Schumacher
180

MACABRE HUMOR
by Reinhold Aman
185

ETHIOPIAN JOKES
by Richard Christopher
188

AIDS JOKES
194

MISCELLANY
196

CONTRIBUTORS
197

INDEX
199

Introduction

Every day around the world, tens of thousands of people are humiliated, demoted, fired, fined, jailed, injured, killed, or driven to suicide because of *maledicta:* insults, slurs, curses, threats, blasphemies, vulgarities, and other offensive words and expressions. *Maledicta* (from Latin, meaning "bad words") cover a broad spectrum of language traditionally shunned in public by prudish professors, prim word-popes, and other properlings who, nonetheless, use many such words in private. *Maledicta* are the opposite of prayer, praise, and flattery, the black sheep of language that most people use but few talk or write about.

Nasty or naughty language is heard most often in stressful, angry, and other emotionally charged situations. It ranges from relatively harmless—but still negative—terms such as "She's no spring chicken" (meaning: she's old) to the vilest language. It is spoken as fluently in ivory towers, in penthouses, and in elegant corporate offices during hostile takeover attempts as it is in the gutter.

There are many types of verbal aggression, from one-word slurs ("chickenbrain") to earthy comparisons ("It's raining like a cow pissing on a flat rock") and sneaky insults that only the in-group understands: a professor who says of a colleague, "He is a good committee man," really means that he is a rotten teacher and researcher.

This anthology, selected by the editors of Running Press from the 2,500 pages of the eight volumes of *Maledicta: The International Journal of Verbal Aggression,* 1977–85, concentrates on the lighter, funnier, more whimsical aspects of our topic. Yet the studies of what people call each other, their blasphemies, and their slang for body parts and excretions are a serious, often sad, matter. Our studies embrace many fields, from anthropology to zoology, and shed much light on human nature, on value systems, and on the psychological, linguistic, and sociological aspects of language. To avoid becoming depressed by the egocentric inhumanity toward others that we encounter in our studies, we cheer up our readers with witty and whimsical pieces about "bad words."

"Bad words" have existed since the first humans bumped their toes, missed their prey, or met hostile members of another prehistoric tribe. But of those one or two million years of *maledicta,* we know only a fraction, not only because there were no written records until some 5,000 years ago, but also because most philologists, linguists, and lexicographers refuse to deal with or record such negative language out of fear of staining their professional image or because of their own puritanical upbringing.

Thus, 22 years ago, I decided to dedicate my life to the collection and analysis of all those words and expressions shunned by academia, and to publish the results in our annual journal, *Maledicta,* with the motto: "They say it—we print it." This specialization has resulted in worldwide recognition and praise, but it has required me to develop a thick skin against the ridicule and damnation by the "cacademics"—those who look up to gynecologists, psychiatrists, and other specialists in human illnesses, but who look down upon the few brave philologists who merely collect and study "dirty" words for "dirty" body parts. To such people, the *word* is more repulsive than the *thing* for which it stands—a strange twist indeed, but common in strait-laced societies. Despite criticism, we will carry on, compelled by a childlike curiosity about human beings, while maintaining sensitivity to their feelings.

In *Maledicta* we have presented many foreign languages (European, Asian, African, and American Indian) and many topics (the secret languages of homosexuals, children, prostitutes, and prisoners), as well as scholarly analyses of terms of copulation and taxonomies for classifying this immense amount of research. Still, in 22 years of investigating some 220 languages from the past 5,000 years, we have only scratched the surface. Therefore, I have embarked upon a 20-year organized study of "bad words" worldwide, using my lengthy "Maledicta Onomastic Questionnaire." This MOQ and its companion, MOQ II, are the basis for our future multi-volume, multi-language *Dictionary of Regional Anatomical Terms*. Anyone interested in having his or her vocabulary eternalized in this dictionary, and willing to contribute several hours to fill out my questionnaires, is invited to request a free copy of MOQ by writing to me at the address below.

The Bible contains more negative language, curses, verbal aggression, and "dirty" topics than *Maledicta,* so don't be too hasty to condemn this anthology. It provides a good-natured look at bad-tempered people the world over, and should make you chuckle and think. True, *Maledicta* is "the journal the world swears by," but enjoying it shouldn't turn you into a mean-mouthed mule-driver. When all else fails, there is nothing more therapeutic than tears or a blue-streaked verbal blast. At all other times it is best to keep a civil tongue. Trust me—I know.

Reinhold Aman, Ph.D.
Editor, *Maledicta*
331 South Greenfield Avenue
Waukesha, Wisconsin 53186

A Word for It!

G. Legman

So you always wanted to write—talk interestingly—swear a blue streak? Well, it's very simple. It's like singing: *if you can talk, you can sing.* All you have to do is know the tune. Nowadays, when both women and men talk very freely, this is more important than it ever was before. For instance, in the mid-Victorian era, a century ago, when Mark Twain's wife foolishly tried to break him of his famous habit of pyrotechnical profanity just after their marriage, by memorizing all his awfullest swear-words and then repeating them back at him over the breakfast table, perhaps one morning in Elmira, New York, on the excuse of some burnt toast. Twain listened carefully to the monotonous and profane tirade, then gravely said: "Olivia, my dear, you know all the words, but you haven't got the *tune.*"

The first thing—even before learning the tune—is to know the right words, and the long colorful phrases too. Don't go to dictionaries, whatever you do; not even to dictionaries of slang. They're all still living out the problem of Mark Twain's wife. And most of them are careful to omit what they consider to be the "dirty words" (still today!) which are invariably the most interesting. Let's begin with those. We can write our own dictionary or arsenal of expressive remarks. It won't be alphabetical, and will go by subjects instead.

Add to these lists the words and phrases I've overlooked or don't know, and that you do. I'd even be very glad if you would send me a copy of your additions. But the main thing is to set down the living words and odd turns of speech you really use and have heard; to go to the grassroots of our own folk speech, to get down to the real linguistic *nitty-gritty;* to *fish or cut bait; high, wide & handsome; shit or get off the pot.* That is how people really talk. The rest is wind.

In the lists that follow, all the words and phrases are generally known and used at the present time throughout the United States, unless they are marked specifically as country or rural dialect, Southernisms, or cowboy and western terms, and the like. Words that are still mostly British slang, though understood in America, are marked (Brit.). All these change and intermingle slowly as time passes. Many slang words and expressions, especially the ones that are very popular and are used too often, go out of style and disappear in a few years, and are rapidly replaced by new ones. The colorful phrases and odd turns of speech last longer. Who makes them up, nobody knows. Is it you by any chance?

All-Purpose Insults

At one time, the question of illegitimacy or bastardy was considered very important as a matter of family honor. Some of the principal insults in the English and other languages for centuries make a special point of this, by implying that one's mother is unchaste or a prostitute: a *bitch*. Consider: *bastard, son-of-a-bitch* (the older *son-of-a-whore* or *whoreson*); also *son-of-a-bitch-of-a-bastard*, which moves the insult up one further generation, and the whole string of adjective forms: *dirty bastard, lousy bastard, stinking bastard*, and more hateful and more colorful variations, such as *cheap phoney-baloney ass-scratching bastard*. Many of these combinations are also used to heighten insults connected with the other person's race, religion, nationality, or unfashionable skin-color. You can fill these in yourself.

Where one was once insulted by being accused of frequenting a *whore*—always pronounced *hoor*, as in the Dutch language from which it comes—and being a *whoremonger*, a *whore-hopper* or a *brothel-creeper* (also a *chippy-chaser*, a *cunt-hound*, a *pimp*, or a *gigolo*, or even a *tit-kisser*, which really just means a seducer), the main accusation of this kind nowadays is of having intercourse with one's own mother: of being a *motherfucker*, originally a Negro term and seldom seriously meant. Incest between brothers and sisters, and fathers and daughters, is quite common in all social classes; but that of mothers and sons is of the greatest statistical rarity and probably always has been. The popularity of *motherfucker* is based precisely on its defying our deepest taboo. There is also a whole lesser spectrum of obviously burlesque and mocking synonyms for the same thing, such as *granny-jazzer, mammy-jammer, momma-hopper,* and *poppa-lopper.* These are used to raise a laugh, not to start a fight.

Curiously enough, the insulting intention in almost all these can be changed or reversed into a rough and grudging compliment by a subtle change in the tone of voice or inflection—the tune—in which they are delivered. *Lucky bastard* and *smart son-of-a-bitch,* or *bad-ass motherfucker* are nowadays terms of sincere admiration. Even *bitch* can become a compliment if said in the right way; a *real bitchen woman* is considered the finest type on the West Coast. Opposite to *fucken,* this is the ultimate.

When you want to call a man a fool or a knave, the choice of available terms is practically unlimited, and in all languages. This is because everything that goes wrong in the world is *somebody else's fault,* and the subject comes up fairly often. Whole dictionaries of these words have been published, especially in the German language which has the most, under the name of *Schimpfwörter.*

In ordinary speech or slang today, a disliked person is often accused of being a masturbator, of not being sexually adult. He may be called a *jerk,* a *jerkoff* or a *jackoff;* a *wank* (Brit.), or a *whack.* He is *whacky,* or *whacked to the gills;* he is *wonked goggle-eyed,* or is suffering from *Wanker's Doom.* The last refer to the old idea or threat that masturbation will make a person go blind or deaf or crazy, owing to the observable fact that the insane often do masturbate without concealment. Another threat, petrified in the mould of words, is that *hair will grow in the palm of your hand,* or *you won't be able to uncurl your pinkie* (the smallest finger). I have heard this said to a woman as a joke, but in general women are seldom accused of masturbation. On the other hand, I once overheard a man fighting with a *diesel-dyke* over a girl they both wanted, who snarled at her: *"Ah, ya big fat clitoris, g'wan home an' give it a rub for me!"*

Disliked or inconvenient persons may be told: *go away and play with yourself,* or more plainly, *go home and jerk off;* or *fuck off, will you? Go piss up a rope and play with the steam* says the same thing. They may be asked: *why don't you go shit in a pot and duck your head?* or simply told to *eat shit!* Or to *get stuffed,* or *go get stuffed with a turkey-neck* or *with a rotten potato.* More ornately: *go shit in your hat and pull it down over your ears—and call it curls!* No one would mistake these for compliments. In his edition of Robert Burns' "Merry Muses of Caledonia," James Barke tells of seeing a young, red-headed Scottish barmaid almost suffocated with shame and embarrassment when a drunk to whom she was required to refuse another drink flung out at her, "with a viciousness that cannot be conveyed in print, *'Then gie me a hair frae your dirty big red cunt!'"*

In America one of the most usual insulting invitations today is *go fuck yourself.* (In England they say *bugger yourself.*) This rather lacks bounce, and is sometimes varied or enlarged to: *go fuck a dead horse*, or *go fuck yourself with a rubber weenie*, or *go fuck yourself in the ass and give yourself some brains*, which allows of the reply or cross-compliment, *I've got more brains in my ass already than you've got in* both *your heads*. Perhaps the most commonly heard is the simple and almost classic invitation or curse: *Fuck you!* This replaces the older reference to hell & damnation in an age of unfaith. It is probably short for *I fuck you*, or *I fuck you in the ass*, a threat or insult that goes back to Ancient Egypt, where the god Min actually carries out this threat on one of his enemies, who then has a baby (Thoth) born from his forehead. The myths of Dionysus being born from Jupiter's thigh—and Eve from Adam's rib—are simply later and more polite versions of this. Egyptian legal documents of the last dynasties used to be reinforced, where today we might have a notary public's seal, with the stereotyped phrase: "As for him who shall disregard it, *may he be fucked by a donkey.*" The hieroglyph for this curse makes the matter unmistakably clear with two little drawings of large, erect penises. This Egyptian cartouche appears as the seal or coat-of-arms of MALEDICTA.

The simplest kind of verbal attack is to accuse another person of low intelligence or lack of culture. Usually this involves scatological images and anatomy, rather than sex. The fool or clod *doesn't know his ass from a hole in the ground*, or *from his elbow*, or *from third base*, or *from a double-barrelled shotgun*. He is *so dumb he couldn't find his ass with both hands at high noon*, or is *too dumb to haul out his jock to piss without a button-hook*, or *don't know how to scratch his ass*. Other rural phrases adding up to the same thing include the accusation that one *doesn't know his butt from a gourd*, or *don't know frog-shit from pea-soup*. Likewise, he *don't know sheepshit from cherry-seed*, or *don't know a mule's ass from a lemon*, or *can't tell owlshit from putty without a map*. He is *so dumb he couldn't pour piss out of a boot—with the directions printed on the heel*. His wife has *marital thrombosis—she's married to a clot*.

Owls are for some reason considered very droll. An inexperienced person is *as green as owlshit*. A backwoodsman or hick *comes from Owl-Shit Junction*, or plainly from *Shitville*. (The cleaned-up version of this is *Mudville*, as in that classic barroom recitation, "Casey At the Bat.") People who flee the big city and its smog, to breathe the pure air of the back-hills, have been known to complain that they are living *so far out in the boondocks that you have to wipe the owlshit off the clock to see what time it is*.

A person that you don't like is often described in terms of various bodily parts or excretions: he is a *prick*, a *schmuck*, a *putz* (Yiddish), an *asshole*; a *fart*, a *snot*, a *shit* (and therefore a *Four-Letter Man*), a *turd*, a *shit-ass* or *shit-head*. If cowardly as well, he is a *piss-willie* or *has shit in his blood*; though a clever person is sometimes called a *piss-cutter*, presumably from the winter duties of bellboys in oldtime country hotels. In general, *he isn't worth wiping your ass on* (politely: *your shoes*), or *ain't worth trading for a shit-ass pup*. He's *not worth a pisspot full of crabapples*, and *don't amount to a fart in a whirlwind*. I think this makes the point very clear. A Spaniard or Mexican might say he is a *pendejo*, a pubic hair.

Moral calibre is considered always in terms of high and low. Low is bad, "feminine," raped, and on the way to Hell. High is on the way to Heaven, and masculine: *top banana* in the pederastic pecking-order of men-among-men. A man of low moral calibre is *lower than the spots on a snake's ass*. He's *so low he can kiss a tumblebug's gilliewinkie without bending his knees*, or can *look up a snake's asshole and think it's the North Star*. All the images here over-define the lack of status and idealism in the person described. At the bottom of the heap is the individual who is *lower than whale-shit—and that's on the bottom of the ocean*.

If he is ugly, *he's got a face like a douche-bag*, or *a toilet-seat*. If he is particularly ignorant or foolish, and proves it by talking loudly or a lot about things he knows nothing about, *his ass is out a yard—and sucking wind. His guts are moving the wrong way*, or *he's doing a lot of shitting and his pants ain't even down yet.* Plainly phrased, he *shits through his mouth*. Also, *he's got his balls twisted*, and *his ass is sucking blue mud*. In fact, *he doesn't know whether to suck or blow*, or *whether to shit or go blind.* If he boasts of his travels he is told: *I've been further around a pisspot looking for the handle than you've been away from home.* If he mentions his family, they're *like an Irishman's fart: always making a lot of noise and raising stink, and never want to go back where they came from.*

If he is fundamentally dishonest and a liar to boot, he's a *bullshitter*, or a *bullshit artist* (*B.A.*). He is *throwing the bull* (or is a *Spanish athlete*), or is *shovelling* or *piling it higher and deeper* (*Ph.D.*). He is accused of *spinning it out of his ass*, like a spider no doubt, and his audience *needs a little ear-scoop to filter out the horseshit*, or lies. One thing is sure: *you can't trust him any farther than you can throw a bull by the prick*, or *than you can see up an alligator's ass in a dust-storm* (or *at midnight*). If he has the nerve to be insulting—a privilege reserved strictly to our side—*his ass is so close to his mouth you can smell the shit on his breath.* Worst of all, *when he has a mouthful of shit he always wants to spit it on you.* We all know people like that.

Someone who is prone to cheat or compete unfairly is now known as a *shaftsman* or *shaft-artist*. He *gives you the shaft*, or *shafts* you. (This was the late President Kennedy's favorite term, but pronounced with an inimitable Harvard accent as *shahfting*.) He *slips it to you where the rhinoceros got the javelin*, or *where the monkey shoved the nuts*, or *where Moby Dick got the old harpoon*. You know what, and you know where. A person like that would *just as soon screw you behind a haystack as say how-de-do*. He's a *real Greek*, or *Turk McGurk*, so don't ever *turn your back on him* or *pick up the soap in the shower with him.*

Things may degenerate rapidly into a face-to-face contest in insults and wild threats. What used to be called "water-wit," because it was most safely engaged in by passengers on riverboats; now by taxicab drivers. *"I don't want to say anything nasty, but one thousand fucking assholes to you!"* — *"Don't open a big mouth at me; I wouldn't shit down your throat if you were starving."* — *"And I wouldn't piss up your rotten guts if you were dying of thirst!"* Young blacks have verbal contests like this in anti-family insults, called *sounding* or *signifying* or "The Dozens," that often end in killings. At these altitudes, artful understatement is often the most effective: *"Well, you may not be dishonest, but I wouldn't trust you alone in a shithouse without a muzzle."*

The disposition of unwanted objects is quite a problem. In the old days one said *to hell with it!* and that was that. Nowadays a person may be told to *stick it* or *stuff it*, or plainly to *stick it up your ass—and holler fire!* This is essentially an unfriendly remark, and may be answered with: *up your gigi*, or *up your fur-lined shit-chute*, or just *up yours—and give it a left-hand turn*. Some of these share their images with ornate forms of the standard insult, *Fuck you!* For example, *up your poopadoop with a giant firecracker*, or *up your bunny with an open umbrella*, or even *up your brown with a Roto-Rooter—and spin it!*

Invitations of this kind are now commonly accompanied with a gesture meaning approximately the same thing, and known as *The Finger*, in which the middle finger is held up with the others curled below. Sometimes the whole hand and arm rise with a reaming, undulating motion while the other hand strikes repeatedly on the upper-arm muscle. This has largely replaced (at least among adults) the older *nose & thumb* gesture, meaning *"Kiss my ass!"* an international invitation. The gesture of the *finger* is of ancient Italian origin, and was known in Roman times as the *digitus impudicus*. Somewhat as in the modern phrase about being *bitched, buggered and bewildered—and far from home:* one has been *Diddled by the Dirty Digit of Destiny*, or *Fucked by the Fickle Finger of Fate*. This format can be applied to a whole alphabet of abuse from A to Z, as in calling something or someone a *Pimple on the Petrified Prong of Progress* or a *Blister on the Bleeding Bloody Bollocks of Biology*, though I have not heard any others.

Often the emotions run so high that one would like to see the other person *dead & damned to hell*, as it once would have been phrased. But nowadays, *goddamn, hell,* and *damnation,* as well as the various names of the deity, have been so overused that few people take them seriously, anyhow not as swearwords. Something stronger is searched for, and many people find it in sexual accusations: that the other person is impotent, a masturbator, and especially that he is a homosexual or has sexual relations with animals: he is a *duck-fucker* or a *pig-sticker.* A favorite threat is that one will perform various oral or anal homosexual acts on the victim against his will, exactly as in the ancient Egypt of the gods Min and Thoth. It is hard to invent new sex acts.

The disliked person is accused of being a *fag* (or *Three-Letter Man*), a *faggot,* a *fairy,* a *pansy,* a *queer,* a *fruit,* a *fluter,* or *the Queen of the Flits in Hoboken.* He has *taken it in his head to make a living,* or *takes it up the ass so deep his ears light up.* In plain English, he is a *cock-sucker* or a *blowjob artist,* and he doesn't even know how to do it well; so *Suck, you son-of-a-bitch —blow is just a figure of speech!* Naturally, he is also a sycophant and toady to the boss: an *ass-kisser,* and an *arsehole-polisher.* He has a *brown nose* and a *fur tongue,* or is a *T.L.* (*tokus-leker*: Yiddish), and the boss's *automatic tongue-wiper.* At the very least his morals are questionable: *he'd steal a rotten doughnut out of a bucket of snot,* and *he'd fuck a snake if somebody'd hold its hips* (or *head*).

At the opposite end of the scale are men who are just too virile or tough for their own or anybody else's good. Army officers of this type are generally nicknamed *Ironballs* or *Old Brass-Ass,* and similar. These appear in newspaper stories about them watered down to *Tuffypants* or other such nambypambyisms. There's a well-known bawdy song about warriors like these called "The Foreskin Fusileers," or "Heroes of the Night," and the matching Australian recitation, "The Bastard from the Bush," reels out a whole litany of cynical variations on the theme of the supertough anti-hero. Where the ordinary guy wants to be a great lover—*a man with a nine-inch prick and a twelve-inch tongue, who can breathe through his ears*—these phallic heroes of the *macho* pose want only to insult, and end up buggering each other. The insults are the verbal equivalent of the act. At the very mildest, they *shit bricks and fart up a storm*, especially when angered, and are *so tough they have to take a wrench and loosen up their nuts at night so they can get some sleep*. The truth is, they are *S. & M.* (sado-masochist) *queens*.

Women

Women are, of course, a very large subject. Whether loved or hated, beautiful or ugly, madonna or prostitute, sexually available or unattainable, there is a word for every type. If she is broad in the beam, she is *built like a brick shithouse* (or *shit brickhouse*); while your diminutive pocket-Venus may be *candy-assed, narrow-assted*, or *pinch-buttocked*, and *no more worth fucking than a sparrow's butt*. She may even *have a case against the city—they built the sidewalks too close to her ass*. If she is just right, she's *got an ass you could plant a flag on*, or *a cunt you could eat with a spoon*: she is *P.E.E.P.* (Perfectly Elegant Eatin' Pussy). On the other hand, if she falls short of the ideal of desirability, well, *I wouldn't fuck her with your prick*, or *with a borrowed pecker*.

If she is willing, she *has hot pants*, she's a *sex job* and will *melt the fat off your bones* (Trinidadian); she is *hotter than a little red wagon*, or *hotter than a bitch-wolf*. She's *pecker-foolish* (Dialect), she's *got fire in her pants*, she's *an angel looking for Peter*, and she *fucks like a mink*. Actually, *she won't let anybody fuck her but her friends—and she ain't got an enemy in the world*. She can *do more tricks on six inches of stiff* (or *limber*) *prick than a monkey on a twenty-foot rope*.

Contrariwise, if she is stingy with her charms, then the shit really begins to fly. In the Ozarks she is a *baked ass*, politely a *baked Alaska*, which is also used innocently in fancy restaurants for a flambé ice-cream pudding. As to her virginity, she is *saving it, sitting on it*, or *planning to take it to Heaven with her*. If she is actually frigid, she's a *wet smack*, an *ice-cube with a hole in it*; she has an *ice-cold crotch* (pronounced *crutch*), and is *sitting on a frozen custard*. Only *a frigid midget with a rigid digit* can handle her *Eskimo pie*. You *couldn't fuck her with a golden prick*, or with the standard ten-foot pole. You'd have to have *a pole ten-foot-six-inches long, and them last six inches better be solid gold!* This suggests that she may be money-minded: she's *going to* make it to the top—*on her back*. She's just a *groupie*, a *screamer-&-creamer*, a *celebrity-fucker*, and a *plaster-caster*, and is going to *screw her way to success* if she has to begin as *third assistant cocksucker at a Mongolian cluster-fuck*.

But perhaps she is less chaste than stuck-up. She *acts like shit wouldn't melt in her mouth*, or she's *so nice she thinks her shit don't stink*, or *thinks she shits lollipops*. Or the trouble may be, *she thinks her ass is ice-cream, and everybody wants a bite*. And she may be absolutely right: *there's many a man would eat a yard of her shit for a lick at her hole*. (This is not recommended.)

Light Bulb Jokes
Variations on a Theme

From our Readers: **How many... does it take to change a light bulb?**

Americans: Six. One to change the bulb, and five to file environmental impact statements. (Told by a Norwegian student)

Americans: One. (As told in Poland)

Californians: None. Californians screw in a hot tub. (A very clever twist!)

Dominatrices: "None, you ugly, sniveling piece of shit — *you'll* do it after I finish flogging you!" (A dominatrix is the superior member of a Bondage & Domination couple)

Gays: Five. One to change the bulb and four to hold the chandelier.

Jewish Princesses: None. They might chip their fingernails.

Law Students: Five. One to hold the bulb and four to kick the ladder out from under him. (Also told of **Republicans**)

Psychiatrists / Psychoanalysts: Only one, but it takes a very long time, and the light has to *really* want to change. (Variant: really *want*)

Puerto Ricans: Three. One to change the bulb and two to hold the radio.

WASPs: Two. One to mix the cocktails and one to call the electrician.

Women's Libbers / Feminists: Five. One to change the bulb and four to write a magazine article about it. (Variants: Ten; nine to write about it. — Six: One to do it, three to write articles for *Ms.* on it, and two to discuss it at the next women's group meeting)

Contributed by: Leonard Ashley, David Axler, Martha Cornog, Frank Esterhill, Joe Fishbein, Richard Lederer, James Sacks *and* David Streiner.

Windy Words
A Glossary of Euphemisms for The Expulsion of Intestinal Gas

Bob Burton Brown

Said a printer pretending to wit:
"There are certain bad words we omit.
It would sully our art
To print the word F...,
And we never, oh, never, say Sh.."

Some people, especially women over forty, simply cannot bring themselves to use the word *fart*. Although this word may be an appropriate Anglo-Saxon expression commonly used in many classics of English literature and today on every school yard in America by even the most innocent of children, it is still considered vulgar and offensive to some folks (especially the editors of big publishing houses and major book distributors). So, it has become a tradition to invent all sorts of euphemisms — most of them silly or childish — to cover the subject; anything to keep from coming right out and saying it.

We often simply let our farts go unnamed, using instead some indirect pronoun reference, such as "it" or "one" or "them" or "those": "Did you do *it*?" – "I let *one* go" – "He has been letting *them* all night" and "He lets *those* all the time."

When we feel we must call them something more specific, our cultural habit has been to give them disgustingly "cute"

Why did God make farts smell?
—*So the deaf can enjoy them, too.*

little names, something palatable to squeamish mothers and amusing to small children. What did you call "them" at your house? Barks? Poots? Smells? Snappers? Sniffles? Stinkies? Toots? Whiffles?

These are, of course, all euphemisms. A euphemism is a figure of speech by which a delicate word or expression is substituted for one which is considered harsh or indelicate. "Breaking wind" and "passing gas" have been the most acceptable euphemisms in literary circles for many years, but these sound so stilted, so old-fashioned, that one almost never hears them in ordinary conversation.

See if you can find your family's favorite euphemism in the following glossary. If not, will you please send it to me, as I would like to add it to this ever-expanding list of "windy words."

bark a sharp report, as in a "barking" gun, makes this a natural for a noisy passage of gas: "Are you barking for your supper or because of it?"

barking spider a gentle, family-type expression to cover the subject in reasonably good humor: "Did I hear a barking spider just now?" or "It's about time to call the exterminators; those barking spiders are back again."

beanie a childish choice, relying on supposition of cause for its identification rather than the end result, as in "Was that your beanie I heard?" or "Do your beanies always smell that bad?"

borborygmus internal farting, the rumbling sounds made by the movement of gas in the intestine, as in a "growling stomach," "belly noise," "gut mumblings," when your stomach "talks to you." Not very useful, since most people will not understand what you are talking about.

bowel howls not really delicate enough to qualify, but nicely descriptive for locker-room talk. Some euphemisms increase rather than ameliorate the impact.

breaking wind very descriptive, and perhaps the most acceptable euphemism in literary circles, but terribly stilted, and dated, too.

Bronx cheer an oral imitation of a sputtering fart, employed to take advantage of a psychological moment which will not wait for the passage of the real thing. Used as a euphemism in "Are you giving me the raspberry?" or "Here's what I think of that...."

bucksnorter a farting hunter who, when tromping through the woods with a buddy, stops, lifts his leg, lets one rip, and then says: "Did you hear that buck snort?"

cushion creeper a muffled fart that seems never to end, and lingers—both the sound and the smell—in, around, and on the soft cushion of an over-stuffed chair or sofa. "I've had about all of your cushion creepers I can take."

cutting the cheese how folks in Indiana describe it when someone lets an especially stinky fart, as in "Cutting the cheese is not allowed in the living room."

elephant on my back an announcement that you are about to let one rip, intended to dupe some gullible fool (or child) into making an innocent inquiry or investigation—then "getting it" with a well-timed blast. Also, one may inquire of a suspected culprit, "Is there an elephant on your back?"

exterminal gas a quasi-technical term coined by my youngest son to describe particularly smelly expulsions of intestinal gas—the kind that could exterminate you, or provide overwhelming evidence that the expulsor is afflicted by something terminal.

flatulence gas with class; whatever fancy folks blow out their ass.

flatus farts with status; a puff of wind; gas generated in the stomach or bowels.

gas or **gassy** mothers who have traditionally had real difficulty bringing themselves to use four-letter Anglo-

Saxonisms often prefer to describe flatulence as "gas," as in "You seem to be awfully gassy today" or "Was that your gas?" or "I just passed some gas."

house frog another family-type term often used to explain the situation nicely, as in "What was that?" – "Just a house frog." – "Okay." An outside equivalent may be found in the question "Who stepped on that frog?" or "Is that damned frog loose again?"

it an all-purpose term for whatever four-letter word we feel we must avoid, as: "Okay, you guys, which one of you did it?" or "It just slipped out."

one what prudes call an expulsion of intestinal gas, as in "Did you just let one?" – "Yes, and that *one* is enough."

one-cheek sneak when little boys in short pants fart while seated on a flat wooden bench or chair.

pain an indirect reference to discomforting flatulence, sometimes used as a euphemism, as in "Did you just have a pain?" Or as a confession in "That was a terrible pain I got rid of."

painting the elevator in a Jewish neighborhood, after you have just let a real stinker on an elevator (thinking you are all alone) and somebody gets on at the next floor, you wrinkle up your nose and say, "They must have just painted this elevator." In our family we all know what it means when one of us asks, "Who painted the elevator?"

passing gas pretty straight-forward, but it always reminds me of a cartoon I saw once of several bicyclists pedaling by a gasoline pump held by a disappointed service station attendant on a lonely highway in the desert, with the caption "Passing Gas."

pets what French-Canadians call farts; and farting is called "petting"—not because they are fond of it, and not to be confused with the pawing of eager lovers; short for the French word *pétard*, meaning "to crack, to explode, to break wind"—in other words, a French fart.

poop a noun, used as a euphemism for anything that comes out of the anus; often a term of pseudo-endearment, as in "You old poop!"

poot an interjection used to express disgust. In the South it is a popular euphemism for fart, especially among the women-folk.

puff as in "a puff of wind," exappropriated as a verb all too often, as in "I hope all those beans we ate for supper don't make us puff all night."

pumping gas a childish euphemism for farting—a confusion of the kind of gas Daddy puts in his car with the kind he puts out of his rear-end.

raspberry the equivalent of "Bronx cheer," a mouth-fart, used as an expression of derision to let others know that you are displeased with them. A spluttering noise made while sticking the tongue out, which translates: "I fart on thee!"

rattler a reverberating blast powerful enough to rattle cups and saucers, or, perhaps, even the windows and doors of rickety buildings—like army barracks.

S.B.D. the abbreviation for the worst kind of fart—the silent-but-deadly; in medical circles, this is called a "tacit" fart.

shooting rabbits what one says Down East when one hears a fart of unknown origin: "Somebody is shooting rabbits!" or "Are you the one that's been shooting rabbits all night?"

silent horror a very smelly fart inflicted upon another without fair warning; illegal chemical warfare, something akin to mustard gas.

smell or **smelly** too obvious to merit comment: "Mommy, I let a smelly."

snappers beans, for obvious reasons; served every Saturday night throughout New England, "to put life into the old boy!" Also used to describe what happens after the beans have had a chance to work.

sniffle the women and children in my ex-wife's family used this word, both as a noun and as a verb, to cover their flatulence as sweetly as possible. Personally, I never liked the term. On my side of the family a "sniffle" was something we blew out of our nose.

sputter sound imitations are sometimes useful: "I've been sputtering (*or* spluttering) all day." However, one can go too far with this if the imitation is too close to the real thing, as in "Who just 'sphtttttt'?"

squeaking chair a clever way to bring the passage of gas to public attention, asking: "Are you sitting in a squeaking chair?" or "I think my chair squeaks." A variation on this theme can be: "Is there a mouse in here?"

stepping on a frog if you have ever stepped on a frog, or can imagine the complaints the frog would give you if you did; no further explanation is necessary.

stink or **stinky** boys let "stinks" but nice little girls call theirs "stinkies."

storm implies a strong and dangerous wind, invariably noisy, as in "Is that your storm I hear?" – "Yes, my stomach is really storming (*or* howling) today."

toot a mild euphemism for a particularly melodious fart. The Yankee equivalent of the South's "poot." Some families use the variation **tootles**.

whiff a windy-sounding term that makes your meaning clear. "Somebody just whiffed; I can smell it!" Variations: **whiffles** and **whiffling**.

wind as in "Was that your wind?" or "I sure feel windy today" or "Standing downwind of you can be dangerous." Sometimes referred to as a **howling wind**.

THANK YOU FOR NOT FARTING

How to Judge People by Their Farting Styles

L. Herrera

Crafty (*taimado*): The person who cuts one and then looks around as if somebody else had done it.
Silly (*tonto*): The guy who cuts farts when he's asleep and gets up to see who knocked at the door.
Surprised (*sorprendido*): Somebody who thought he was letting one out silently but has it come out thundering.
Expert (*perito*): The fellow who can tell his own from somebody else's even when they smell at the same time.
Eloquent (*elocuente*): The person whose farts make people gather around to listen.
Honest (*honrado*): The guy who cuts them loudly and openly.
Lovesick (*enamorado*): The fellow who delights in breathing his girlfriend's farts.
Perspicacious (*perspicaz*): The person who can tell by the smell what the perpetrator had eaten and the name of the restaurant.
Good Businessman (*comerciante*): The guy who lets farts in monthly installments.
Well-bred (*educado*): The person who holds a fart even though he's all alone, just out of consideration for himself.
Simpleton (*simple*): The guy who cuts farts in the bathtub and gets a big charge out of the bubbles they make.
Unlucky (*desafortunado*): The individual who lets rip-roaring big farts.
Cautious (*precavido*): The fellow who lets them out gently so his shorts won't get torn.
Musically Inclined (*filarmónico*): The guy who can perform ascending and descending scales.
Dumb (*estúpido*): The fellow who enjoys somebody else's fart thinking it was his own.
Joker (*comodino*): The guy who lifts his butt so he can cut one at will.
Strategist (*estratégico*): The person who knows how to disguise a fart by sneezing or making some other opportune noise.
Curious (*curioso*): When this fellow cuts a fart in a cane-bottom chair, he squats down to see which hole it came out.

Poonerisms

Richard Christopher

Most of us know somebody who occasionally says *revelant* for *relevant*, *pasghetti* for *spaghetti*, or *aminal* for *animal*. In each of these mispronunciations there is a switching of sounds between the two words; the scientific name for this phenomenon is *metathesis*, from the Greek meaning "transpose."

In English we call the intentional or unintentional transposition of letters, syllables, or words a *spoonerism*, named after the Rev. William Archibald Spooner (1844-1930), once warden of New College, Oxford. Spooner is said to have set out to become a *bird watcher* and instead to have ended up as a *word botcher*.

The first of Spooner's spoonerisms, and one of the few that have been authenticated, was spoken by the great man in 1879, when he was conducting a service at the College and announced the hymn as "*K*inkering *K*ongs Their Titles Take." Other switches attributed to Spooner (most of them spuriously) include: "Three cheers for our *q*ueer old *d*ean!" (referring to Queen Victoria); "Is it *k*istomary to *c*uss the bride?"; "Stop *h*issing all my *m*ystery lectures"; "You are occu*pew*ing my *pie*"; and "The Lord is a *Sh*oving *L*eopard."

Spoonerisms have become a prolific source of American folk humor, and many children cut their punning eyeteeth on a special form of riddle called the "What's the difference between..." question:

What's the difference between a mouse and a pretty girl?
— *One harms the cheese; the other charms the he's.*

What's the difference between a tube and a crazy Dutchman?
— *One is a hollow cylinder, the other a silly Hollander.*

What has seldom been noted or explored is the fact that spoonerisms play a major role in the formation of bawdy jokes, a phenomenon that would have little pleased the good reverend. For what I hope are obvious reasons, I would call such bawdy transpositions *poonerisms*. Here is a sampling of my favorite poonerisms, with an indication of each transfer:

> What's the difference between a pickpocket and a peeping Tom?
> — *One snatches watches; the other watches snatches.* (Word transfer)

> What's the difference between a nun at vespers and a nun in the bathtub?
> — *One has hope in her soul, the other soap in her hole.* (Letter transfer)

> What's the difference between a magician and a chorus line?
> — *The magician has a cunning array of stunts...* (Letter transfer)

> What's the difference between pigmies and female track stars?
> — *Pigmies are cunning runts...* (Letter transfer)

> What's the difference between an epileptic oysterman and a whore with diarrhea?
> — *One shucks between fits...* (Letter transfer)

> Definition of a pimp: a snatch purser. (Syllable transfer)

> Prostitute to customer: "It's been a business doing pleasure with you." (Word transfer)

> A midget was fired from the circus for sticking his nose in everybody's business. A tall man was fired from the circus for sticking his business in everybody's nose. (Word transfer)

> Radio blooper: "Good evening, ladies and gentlemen, and welcome to another evening with the Canadian Broadcorping Castration." (Syllable transfer)

What do you call a drink made of 7-Up, grenadine, and cyanide?
— *The Shirley People's Temple.*

The son of a shah is called a shan. A certain shan was afflicted with epilepsy. One day, the shan, moving amongst his harem, was smitten with a seizure. When his attendants arrived shortly thereafter, the harem girls inquired of them: "Where were you when the fit hit the shan?" (Letter transfer)

And, finally, the classic set-up poonerism:

A hunter was out shooting game in the wilds of Africa. When he came to a certain part of the jungle, all of his native bearers bolted in panic, save one—his most faithful companion. When the hunter asked the remaining bearer why the others had fled, he replied: "You are about to enter the territory of the Great and Terrible Foo Bird. The Foo Bird has sixty-four teeth and a hundred-foot wingspan, but the worst thing is that, if you step on his turf, he will shit on your head. And if you wipe it off, you die."

"Bosh," replied the hunter, and took another step. Immediately the sky darkened as the Great and Terrible Foo Bird swooped down and planted a huge turd on the hunter's head.

Afraid to wipe off the Foo Bird pat that now sat upon his head, the hunter lived with it for five years. But it stank horribly and had an incredibly long half-life. Finally, the hunter could stand the stench no longer and proceeded to wipe off the turd.

And his head fell off, and he died.

Moral: *If the Foo shits, wear it.* (Letter transfer)

Three proofs that Jesus was black:
—*(1) He called everybody "brother"; (2) He had no permanent address; (3) Nobody would hire him.*

Three proofs that Jesus was a Californian:
—*(1) He never cut his hair; (2) He walked around barefoot; (3) He founded a new religion.*

Three proofs that Jesus was an Italian:
—*(1) He talked with His hands; (2) He had wine at every meal; (3) He worked in the building trades.*

Why is the ERA an impossible dream?
—*Because there will always be a* vas deferens *between men and women.*

The Cockney's Horn Book
The Sexual Side of Rhyming Slang

Leonard R.N. Ashley

Slang as a word came into English (from slang itself) before 1756, when it was first recorded. As a lively linguistic phenomenon, slang has been with us much longer, as the *Dictionary of the Canting Crew* and *A New Canting Dictionary* (both in the first half of the Eighteenth Century) testify. With Grose's *Dictionary of the Vulgar Tongue* (first published in 1785 and frequently reprinted), slang came into its own and in our century has attracted such experts as the redoubtable Eric Partridge. Dr. Johnson ponderously pontificated that "of the laborious and mercantile part of the people the diction is in great measure casual and mutable," but it is in their slang that they show their genius.

I have written extensively on British slang for food and drink and money and now wish to offer a brief article on another necessity, sex. Other articles on British sexual slang will follow, but here I shall limit myself to rhyming slang. I do not mean *claptrap, sure cure,* and *hot shot* (though sexual meanings attach to *AC/DC, rough stuff,* and so on) but the Cockney rhyming slang that involves *apples* (*apples and pears* = 'stairs') and *Bristols* (*Bristol City* = 'tittie'). Use your *loaf* ('head').

In "Rhyme and Reason: The Methods and Meanings of Cockney Rhyming Slang, Illustrated with Some Proper Names and Some Improper Phrases" (*Names* XXV, No. 3, September 1977, 124-154) I examined chiefly those examples which de-

---

What's a Behavioral Psychologist?
—*One who pulls habits out of rats.*

rive from proper names. These included some sexual slang:

A comedy in the vulgar, popular "Carry On" series was called *Carry On Up the Khyber*, hinting to the informed who recognize that *Khyber Pass* (famous from the days of the British *raj* in India) rhymes with *ass*. . . . No use objecting that the Cockney says *arse* and that it does not rhyme; how do you think he pronounces *pass*? (A Spanish teacher telling an East London class to "roll your r's" is asking for trouble. . . .)

* * *

On BBC television on October 29, 1975 they [the comedy team of Morecambe and Wise] gave us this little exchange:

I grew spices for a man in India.
Ginger?
No, he was married.

Got it? No? Well, *ginger beer* = 'queer.'

* * *

But who can cope with *trolley* = 'copulate' (from *trolley and truck*, in a country where our truck is a van!) . . . .

* * *

Oh, my sister's name is Tilly,
She's a whore in Picadilly,
And my mother is another in The Strand.
And my brother peddles arsehole
At the Elephant and Castle.
We're the finest f——ing family in the land.

The fact that the slang contains other meanings for *elephant*, or that *au fond* there are plenty of terms for 'bottom'—*bottle* (and glass), *North Pole* ('hole'), and *Khyber* (as we have said)—deters no one. The peculiar Cockney pronunciation of *castle* (carsole) is to be found also in rhyming slang such as *Crimea* ('beer'), *Balaclava, chaver*. . . .

Then I had to explain that *chaver* = 'sexual intercourse', perhaps derived from the French *chauffer* ("to heat up") or the Romany *charvo* ("to fool around"). These foreign tongues are rather complicated!

The concentration in that article on proper names produced theatrical names (*J. Knowles* = 'holes'; *Tommy Dodd* = 'sod', as in sodomy and *sod off* = 'fuck off'; *Beattie & Babs* = 'crabs', including the word as used for body lice; and *Mae West* = 'breast'), play titles (as *Colleen Bawn* = 'horn', that is 'erection', also *Marquis of Lorne*) and people's titles (*Duke of Kent* = 'bent', which is the equivalent of the American *twisted* sexually but not as queer as *kinky*), etc. Place-names turned up (*Burton* [on Trent] = *rent*, 'a male hustler'; *Hampton Wick* = 'prick', with "He gets on my wick" for the US "He bugs me"; and *Niagara* [Falls] = 'balls', but in the sense of UK *rubbish* and US *bullshit*, not 'testicles'—those are *bollocks, fun and frolics*, and *cobblers* [awls]—the latter serving for both *bollocks* and *bullshit*). Also in evidence were department stores in London such as *C & A* = 'gay' (homosexual)—with "Cocksucker and Arsehole" explaining the initials—and *Barker's* = *starkers* ('nude', US *stark naked*). Literature provided *Friar Tuck* = 'fuck', and horses both *Berkeley Hunt* = 'cunt' (in the sense of "you stupid cunt," not a synonym for *vagina*—often "you stupid *berk*") and *Harry Wragg* = 'fag', after a once-famous jockey, but *fag* in the sense of cigarette, not US faggot—for which the UK is *pouf* or *poufter, nancy, fairy*, etc. *Beggar boy's* [ass] is not sexual: it means Bass (ale). More examples are *Pat and Mick* = 'prick', *Rory O'More* = 'whore' (also *scrubber, slag*, etc.), and *Alphonse* = *ponce* ('pimp'). The article went into detail about linguistic and historical matters and attempted to demonstrate that in Cockney Rhyming slang's onomastic aspects we have one more example of the "richness, good sense, and terse convenience" for which Jakob Grimm praised the English language.

There are other, more general if less modern and correct, studies of Cockney rhyming slang, though they tend to skirt *Tom Tit* ('shit'), *rattle* [and hiss] ('piss'), *you and me* ('pee') and *me and you* ('screw', which in England often means *pay packet* or *wages* but has come to mean, as in the US, 'fuck', *stuff*, even *bugger*). To Julian Franklyn's standard book *The Cockney* have been added an anonymous *Dictionary of Rhyming Slang* (published by John Langdon, London, 1941) and little books such as Bob Aylwin's *A Load of Cockney Cobblers* (1973) and the even smaller *Rhyming Cockney Slang* (1971, edited by Jack Jones). From these we may garner some rhyming slang on sexual matters not covered in my onomastics article.

Mr. Aylwin has a two-page section on "Vulgarity." Too brief, and he occasionally is unreliable: *elephant* [and castle] is not "arse" but the rhyming "arsehole." To *Berkeley Hunt*, however, he is able to add these other words for *cunt*, though he mixes up the terms used to describe female anatomy and those used only as insults (stupid *berk*): *gasp & grunt, growl & grunt, Joe Hunt, sharp & blunt.* He misses the acting duo of *The Lunts* and *junta = cunter* 'playboy', *ass-bandit*, formerly *molrower* (now obsolete, like so many other vivid sex terms: *swive, Athenian, ell*, etc. — Partridge has a charming book on *Shakespeare's Bawdy*). He gives us several terms for tits/titties (*Bristol Cities, cat and kitties, Tale of Two Cities*) and balls (*coffee stalls, orchestra stalls,* and *flowers and frolics,* as he has it for *bollocks*) and also lists:

All forlorn Horn	*Giggle Stick* Prick	*Levy & Frank* Wank
Bang & Biff Syph [ilis]	*Gypsy's Kiss* Piss	*Mad Mick* Prick
Beattie & Babs Crabs	*Hampton Wick* Prick	*Manchester Cities* [Titties
Bottle & Glass Arse	*Hanson Cabs* Crabs	*Marquis of Lorne* Horn
Coachman on the Box Pox	*Hit & Miss* Piss	*Pat & Mick* Prick
Colleen Bawn Horn	*Jodrell Bank* Wank	*Threepenny Bits* Tits
Cream Crackers Knackers [balls]		*Khyber Pass* Arse

Some problems: *Bang* usually means 'fuck' (often 'fuck hard', which in UK is *fuck rotten*), so one would always have to add the *& Biff*, while some of the other expressions (he does not indicate which) omit the rhyming word; *horn* requires the explanation we have given above; and some of the expressions require notes (Jodrell Bank is an astronomical observatory, though Aylwin marks it "R.H.A."—Royal Horse Artillery?). It has to make *eighteen pence* ('sense') to non-native speakers.

Elsewhere Aylwin lists a few more "Vulgarities": *Samuel Hall* ('ball'), words for breasts (*brace and bits, east and west, Jersey City, thousand pities, towns and cities, fainting fits*), whore (*boat and oar*), queer (*Brighton Pier*, though often in the sense of "peculiar" rather than what Aylwin calls a "puff", *collar and cuff*), pimp (*fish and shrimp*), love (*heavens above*), kiss (*hit or miss* again), geezer (*ice cream freezer*, a *geezer* being an old man in common parlance but a *client* to a *rent boy*), spunk (*Maria Monk, spunk* meaning courage as in US "full of spunk" but equivalent to sperm or *cum* in some British circles), bitch (*Miss Fitch,* the opposite of masculine *butch* in *camp* homosexual slang), *nancy* (*tickle your fancy*, a *homo*), and others which are *two thirty* ('dirty'). He gives both *two by four* and *six to four* for 'whore.'

Jack Jones adds *band in the box* (*pox*), *fife and drum* (*bum*, as in posterior, an example of the nursery lingo which gives us *ta* = thank you and *pee* = piss), *iron hoof* ('pouf'), *Nervo and Knox* ('pox', from part of the old Crazy Gang vaudeville team), etc. His *oily rag* ('fag') is a cigarette.

Since "Ducange Anglicus" and his *The Vulgar Tongue* (1857), which noted some still current examples (such as *barnet* = 'hair', from *Barnet Fair*), rhyming slang has been of interest to the general public in England. (Even in America we have picked up examples you may not have noticed as such: *brass tacks* = facts in "let's get down to brass tacks" and *sorry* [and sad] = bad in "what a sorry sight.") In Britain there are fairly frequent journalistic articles on rhyming slang. We may cite "Slang It to Me in Rhyme" in the *Daily Telegraph* (December 17, 1971). There "vulgarities" are restrained but we find: *Alan Whickers* = 'knickers' (women's panties), the Barrow Boy's donkey *barrey moke* = *poke* ('fuck'), *Bristol Cities* = 'breasts' (titties, of course), *Brahms 'n' Liszt* = "inebriated" (*pissed*), *fainting fits* = 'the bosom', *ginger beer* = 'queer' (not as in peculiar), *oily rag* = 'fag' (apparently unaware of the non-smoking variety), and *padlock* = "anatomy again" ('cock', penis). *Tale of Two Cities* is glossed as "a literary approach to the human form divine this time" and *Tom Thumb* (*bum*) as "also, but the rear as opposed to the front projections." *Brahms* can also mean 'urinated' as well as 'drunk' (*pissed as a newt* or *harry flakers*, which is 'half drunk'). Whickers is known for a BBC-TV travelogue of recent vintage (though *Errol Flynn* = 'chin', *Vera Lynn* = 'gin', and murderer *Dr. Crippen* = 'dripping', as in cookery rather than in the clap, have stayed in the language though they have passed out of the news). The *Telegraph* author's shyness (or his editor's) seems to prevent him from speaking more to our purpose. He also finds it convenient to deny much familiarity with things *yank*: *Mutt and Jeff* = 'deaf' he says is "popular, but oddly enough based on an American [comic] strip cartoon (I think)," while he doesn't seem to recognize the American origin of *George Raft* ('draught'), *Mickey Mouse* ('house'), *Raquel Welch* ('belch'), and so on.

This pose is at least as old as Capt. Francis Grose's Preface to his dictionary of 1785 in which he stresses that the author,

> when an indelicate or immodest word has obtruded itself for explanation, ... has endeavoured to get rid of it in the most delicate manner possible; and none has been admitted but such as could not be left out without rendering the work incomplete, or in some manner compensate by their wit for the trespass committed on decorum.

The result has been too much neglect of the often witty slanguage of the Cockneys (and others) and in rhyming slang false modesty about words that simply look as if they might be sexual: *cock* [linnet] = 'minute', not to mention expressions such as *old cock* (buddy, *mate*), *standing peter* (we say "standing pat"), *peter that* ('shut up'), or even *pissing down with rain* ('raining cats and dogs'). One rejoices in *Maledicta*'s frank interest in words that are a vital part of our linguistic heritage. "Who else will tell you these things?" I, for one, propose to continue my onomastic and other linguistic studies in British and American sexual slang and hope to fill more of these pages in *Maledicta* in the future with articles on the difference between US and UK "low" vocabularies, "Kinky English" (British terms for sexual perversions), "Get you, Mary" (the use of proper names in *camp* slang), and studies of *poufs* and *dykes* and *aunties* and *chickens* and *flashers* and *leather queens* and other denizens of the sexual subcultures. The next installment may possibly deal with the salty language of *scrubbers, rent, drag queens,* and the ladies who advertise in London corner shops "Chest For Sale" and "Miss Fifi Gives French Lessons." If you see me in low dives—"I'm writing a book."

What has two million legs and can't walk?
—*Jerry Lewis's kids.*

How do you know when a Negro has been properly baptized?
—*When the bubbles stop rising to the surface.*

Is French a Sexist Language?
Doing Cunteries in France

Andrew R. Sisson

France beckons to us eternally. Alpine skiing at Chamonix or Val d'Isère. A Norman castle or a Loire château. The azure Riviera. And Paris calls us at any time of the year.

Ah, *la belle France*, cultural mother of us all! Seat of rational thought, of refined eating, drinking and fashion in the modern world. Even etiquette itself — good manners as a ticket of entry to sophistication and wealth — is a French invention, although surely the Orientals have their own view of the matter. But beware, you not-so-cunning linguists, of the French tongue as she is really spoken. You are in for a major culture shock, even in the swinging, open eighties. Take out your pocket dictionary — but first of all — listen! In France nowadays, it is fashionable slang among the younger set, whether jet-smart or street-smart, to call everybody a "cunt." Yes, a cunt, or *con*, meaning a stupid or dumb person of either sex. Anti-feminist? Not at all. *Il est con; elle est con; ça, c'est vraiment con* have no sexual cunnotation. They simply mean "dumb" or "stupid." And liberated French girls use this all-purpose noun/adjective just as frequently as their brothers. In the ultra-sophisticated French cartoons of Claire Bretécher, *Les Frustrés*, formerly seen in *MS* and in *Esquire* and recently published in book form in English, the liberated ladies say *con* with great regularity. (The dictionary adjectives for "dumb" are *bête* and *stupide*, but they are seldom used.)

What do you get when you cross a rooster with an M&M?
—*A cock that melts in your mouth, not in your hand.*

Con is not an insult in our English sense. For *us* to call someone a "cunt" or a "dumb cunt" constitutes a crude sexist remark. One envisages a void, ambulatory vagina. After all, are men "cunts" or women "pricks"? We smile at the absurdity. No way. And English has a variety of put-down vocabulary to delve into. Examples:

A. Profanity: *goddamn, Jesus Christ*
B. Dubious ancestry references: *son of a bitch, bastard*
C. Barnyard words: *ass, shit, piss, fuck*
D. Recent Yiddish enrichments: *schlemiel, schnook, schmuck.*

Most recently we have been using *cunt* in a sexy way, in the tell-it-like-it-is prose of today. A sexy genital reference, as in "her hairy, bushy, warm, wet, soft *cunt.*" Not a *person* cunt, but an *organ* cunt. Much nicer than a collective "bunch of cunt" or the "wet split beaver" of Garp's fantasies in John Irving's novel.

How then can the French be so crude, so gross? *Il est con, elle est con, c'est un vrai con.* How can these supposed masters or mistresses of all things refined and cultivated talk that way? Didn't they practically invent sex as a recreational sport in Europe? Aren't "French kissing" and "Frenching" their discoveries? No, but we like to give them credit—or blame—just as national or ethnic chauvinism leads the English to call the male prophylactic a "French letter" and the Gallic cousins to dub same rubber sheath *capote anglaise*, "English raincoat." As in the following ditty, spoken by *madame* or *mademoiselle*:

> **Chéri, quand tu me baises**
> **Ne porte pas la capote anglaise:**
> **Quand tu termines, c'est tellement doux**
> **De sentir couler les bons jus.**

> Darling, when you fuck me
> Don't wear a rubber:
> When you finish it's so sweet
> To feel the good juices flow.

Needless to say, the lady is not talking about roast beef with gravy, au jus.

We know that "cunt" and *con* derive from the Latin *cunnus* (vulva) and *cuneus* (wedge), as in "cuneiform" or wedge-shaped writing. But most of the younger French who call each other *con* are apparently unaware of this fact, or of the fact that *con* refers literally to female genitalia. In any case, listen for the ubiquitous little syllable (sounds like "cawn," more or less) on your next trip to Gaul. French youth has a far richer slang than we—or the Germans—for everyday activities, such as eating, drinking, working or sleeping. Teenagers can talk for hours in a tongue almost incomprehensible to their elders, to say nothing of foreign visitors. Frequently heard expressions include *vachement*, *mec*, and *chiant*, best translated as "terribly," "guy/dude," and "shitty." French is far too heavily salted and peppered, nevertheless, by that overused wordlet *con*. It is perhaps even more prevalent than the World War II American all-purpose adjective *fucking*, and its British equivalent, *bloody*. (*Bloody* comes from "by our Lady" and is thus profane in origin, but its users remain, for the most part, blissfully ignorant of such sources.) The French have another word for vulva as "pussy": it is *chatte*, or female cat, proving that visions of vulvas as feline and furry leap over language barriers. As for the French origin of *bastard*, they use this noun (*bâtard*) very seldom and in its literal sense of illegitimacy, or as a synonym for *petit pain* or small loaf of bread.

Variations on the theme of *con* abound, and you will hear them in ski lines, in village cafés, on beaches, and especially where the language of youth is spoken—in films, on TV, in magazines and novels. *Elle fait des conneries. Il fait des conneries.* How marvelous! "To make cunteries," meaning 'to do stupid things.' In true Gallic logic, *le con*, "cunt," is masculine and *la bitte*, "prick," is feminine; but no matter. There's no logic in language.

Potentiation of a Spanish Insult

Mario E. Teruggi

Hijo de puta, "son of a whore," is undoubtedly the most common personal insult in Spanish, and it is found in the classical literature of Spain as the contracted form *hideputa*. Of course, the formula is found in other languages, either straight or edulcorated, like *son of a bitch*, *son of a gun* and similar expressions in English.

In *hijo de puta* the emphasis is placed on the person whose mother is accused of having been a harlot; but, very often, the interest is displaced towards the mother herself, and the insulting formula is changed to *la puta que te parió*, "the whore that bore you." The English translation is very weak because there is no satisfactory equivalent of *parir*, since "to bear, to give birth, to foal" or "to calve" all lack the force and feeling of rudeness of the Spanish verb.

La puta que te parió, at least in Argentina, is now more frequently heard than *hijo de puta*. With the minor change of the dative pronoun *te* for the neuter *lo* (*la puta que lo parió*), it has an everyday use to discharge one's wrath, annoyance or ill humor against all sorts of inanimate objects, minor accidents or difficulties that stand in our way. The sentence is often reduced to a mere ¡*Que lo parió!* which is also employed to denote surprise or astonishment.

The frequent use of *la puta que lo parió* has, pebble-like, reduced much of its aggressiveness by the rounding off of its cutting edges and corners. That is the reason why, when we are really mad at somebody, we resort to two insults in order to give full vent to our indignation, saying in the same breath ¡*Hijo de puta y la puta que te parió!* It is to be observed that the equivalents of *motherfucker* and *motherfucking* are not

---

A "residential complex" developer in Spain's **Peñiscola**, Vinaroz, urges us to move there. (Advertisement in *L'Express*, Paris, 1 Nov. 1980, p. 57) — *I'll drink to that!* Ed.

used in Spanish, although they would be perfectly understood and can be heard in Mexico (¡Chinga tu madre!, etc.).*

Luckily for the people who want or need to utter their verbal aggressions with superlative strength, the Spanish language offers the possibility of raising the insult to a higher power, so to speak. In Argentina the maximum reinforcement is found in the utterance ¡La reputísima madre que te recontra mil parió! which requires some explaining.

The prefix re-, as in English and many other languages, is used in Spanish to imply repetition or duplication. Putísima is the superlative of puta, here used as an adjective to be translated as "most whorish." La reputísima madre then means "twice the (your) most whorish mother." As to recontra, it means "twice against" (you is implied) and is commonly used as a reply to an insult by simply muttering que te recontra, connoting "the same to you but twice." In the insult we are here considering, as a final reinforcement, the noun mil, "one thousand," is added to recontra.

Thus, the whole sentence can be translated: "The twice most whorish mother that bore you again and again one thousand times!"

In a mathematical approximation, if W stands for "whorish" and B for "bore," the insult formula would be:

$$\text{Insult} = 2 \times W^2 \text{ mother} \ldots B\ (1+1) \times (1000)$$

Actually, (1+1) × (1000) is not understood in the sense that the mother gave birth 2000 times to the same child but as a definite reinforcement of the mother's whorishness.

In a nutshell: the mother that bore you was twice 2000 times squared a whore.

One wonders if other tongues have this possibility of numerically increasing common insults. Of course, one could simply say, "Your mother was a billion times a whore," but it is the multiplying, doubling and squaring that, in a long crescendo, fills the utterer's mouth with a resounding and cathartic sonority.

---

*Larry M. Grimes. 1971. El Tabú Lingüístico: Su Naturaleza y Función en el Español Popular de México. Cuernavaca, CIDOC Cuaderno Nº 64.

Italian and Venetian Profanity

Giuliano Averna

[*Editor's Note:* The following are the most important swearwords, blasphemies, imprecations, and insults in use throughout Italy today. They were collected and translated into English by G. Legman in Venice (March 1977) from the information provided by the Italian poet Giuliano Averna. — Venetian dialect is indicated by (Ven.), Florentine dialect by (Flo.). — Travelling in Italy, I also heard *Ostia Madonna!* Host Madonna! and *Ostia Madonna, matrona di bordello!* Host Madonna, whorehouse madam! — It would be appreciated if some reader could provide more information on the puzzling blasphemies formed with *Faust* and *icecream*.]

1. Swearwords and Blasphemies

Ostia!	Host!
Dio cane!	That dog of a God!
Dio porco!	That pig of a God!
Porco Dio!	That pig of a God!
Dio prete!	That priest of a God!
Dio mottarello!	God icecream!
Cristo!	Christ!
Dio Cristo!	Christ God!
Per Dio!	By God!
Dio boia!	Hangman God!
Dio Faust!	God Faust!
Boia Faust!	Hangman Faust!
Cristo nudo!	Naked Christ!
Puttana Eva!	That bitch (whore) of Eve!
Porca Eva!	That sow of Eve!
Porca Madonna!	That sow of the Virgin Mary!
Madonna puttana!	That bitch of Virgin Mary!
Madonna troia!	That sow of Virgin Mary!
Madonna bucaiola! (Flo.)	That bitch of Virgin Mary!
Madonna damigiana* e tutti i santi per tappo! (Flo.)	That big crock of a Virgin Mary with all the saints as corks!

Madonna damigiana con tutti That big crock of a Virgin
   i santi dentro e Dio per tappo! Mary with all the saints
   (Flo.) inside and God for a cork!

2. Insults

Vai a fare in culo!	Go fuck in the arse!
Và a fà 'n culo! (jargon)	Go fuck in the arse!
Vai in mona! *	Go fuck!
Và 'n mona! (Ven.)	Go fuck!
Và 'n mona de to mare! (Ven.)	Go fuck your mother!
Và 'n mona de to sorela! (Ven.)	Go fuck your sister!
Và 'n figa! * (Ven.)	Go fuck!
Và 'n figa de to mare! (Ven.)	Go fuck your mother!
Và 'n figa de to sorela! (Ven.)	Go fuck your sister!
Vai in culo!	Go fuck in the arse!
Và 'n culo de to mare! (Ven.)	Go bugger your mother!
Và 'n culo de to sorela! (Ven.)	Go bugger your sister!
Vai a fartelo mettere in culo!	Go get fucked in the arse!
Vai a farti chiavare!	Go get fucked!
Và a farte ciavar! (Ven.)	Go get fucked!
Vai a farti fottere!	Go get fucked!

   *Notes: *Damigiana* from French *dame-jeanne* (English *demijohn*) "a large bottle." *Mona* and *figa, fica,* are the two principal Italian slang words for the female genitals.

How do you say "Preparation H" in Italian?
— *Innuendo.*

What's the difference between *ignorance* and *apathy*?
—*I don't know and I don't care.*

Italian Blasphemies

Giuliano Averna and Joseph Salemi

I

Swearing and cursing are very common in Italy. Although the practice is impolite, and a sin in the eyes of religion, most Italians — regardless of their social level — frequently use blasphemy. Perhaps centuries of religious domination, both temporal and spiritual, in extremely close proximity to the central power of the Catholic Church, have driven them to it.

We are all well aware that there are many ways to exorcize something hostile or inimical to us. When we speak of death we are exorcizing it. When we talk more or less freely about homosexuality we often relieve our anxiety concerning the subject. When we refer casually to the signs of age on our bodies, we exorcize our fear of old age and perhaps death itself. In a similar manner, Italians have traditionally cursed and sworn as a means of verbal exorcism, and they continue to do so today.

For centuries blasphemy was the only way of escaping the legal, moral, and inquisitorial power of the priest, the confessor, and the preacher. In the midst of a life of privations these clerics told, counselled, and ordered the wretched majority of the populace to continue suffering and

---

Why did the Italian staple his nuts together?
— *Since he couldn't lick them, he joined them.*

What is *X / X-ski*?
— *A Polack co-signing for a nigger.*

obeying in the hope of a heavenly reward. Meanwhile, the dream of a land flowing with milk and honey was realized daily in the castles and palaces of the rich.

God is clearly the catalyst for the majority of these blasphemies, but we also find expressions that mention Christ, the Madonna, the sacraments, and so on. I have listed here about one hundred expressions in which God's divinity is blasphemed or insulted, along with some euphemisms. They have all been collected from the Italian language and its various dialects.

II
Abbreviations:

cal. dialect of Calabria
emil. dialect of Emilia
ferr. dialect of Ferrara
lig. dialect of Liguria
mil. dialect of Milan
par. dialect of Parma
rom. dialect of Rome
sic. dialect of Sicily
tosc. dialect of Tuscany
ven. dialect of Veneto
venez. dialect of Venice
veron. dialect of Verona

Dio assassino! *That assassin of a God!*

Dio 'ssasino! (ven.) *That assassin of a God!*

Dio beco! (ven.) *Horned God! God with a beak!* This imprecation refers to the horns of cuckoldry. The blasphemy would then have the same force as **Dio cornuto!** *Beco* (Venice, Veneto) and *becco* (standard Italian): "he-goat"; "beak"; "cuckold."

Dio bestia! (ven.) *That beast of a God!*

Dio bestialone! *That big beast of a God!* In Italian the suffix *-one* is a pejorative addition that connotes both largeness and derogation.

Dio birbo! (ven.) *That rascal of a God!*

Dio bonino! (tosc.) *Good God!*

Dio brigante! (ven.) *That bandit of a God!* Brigands and bandits have always been a part of Italian life.

Brigante de Dio! (ven.) *That bandit of a God!*

Dio brutt! (emil.) *Ugly God!*
Dio brutto! (ven.) *Ugly God!*
Dio buono! *Good God!*
Dio campanile! (venez.) *That bell tower of a God!* In Venice and Veneto, *campanile* is also pronounced *canpanile*.
Dio cane! *That dog of a God!*
Dio can! (ven.) *That dog of a God!*
Can de Dio! (mil.) *That dog of a God!*
Dio 'hane! (tosc.) *That dog of a God!*
Dio can-arino! (ven.) *That canary of a God!* This and the following two items are examples of verbal stops, designed to suggest *cane* "dog."
Dio can-oro! (ven.) *That singer of a God!*
Dio can-tante! (ven.) *That singer of a God!*
Dio cara! (ven.) *Dear God!*
Dio caro! (ven.) *Dear God!*
Dio cangi! (lig.) *Dear God!*
Dio cornuto! *Cuckolded God!* See **Dio beco!**
Dio culattiere! (venez.) *That sodomite of a God!* From *culatta*, the rump, the seat of the pants.
Dio fiol! (ven.) *That son of a God!*
Dio ladro! (ven.) *That thief of a God!*
Dio mamma! (ferr.) *That mother of a God!* "Mother" in this imprecation should be understood in the literal sense, not as the shortened form of *motherfucker*, a meaning which the term almost always carries in American malediction.
Dio madonna! *That Madonna of a God!*
Dio mas-cio! (ven.) *That boy of a God!* Another verbal stop, perhaps to suggest the term *mascalzone* "rogue, blackguard." *Mas-cio* also means "pork."
Dio mat! (ven.) *That madman, lunatic of a God!*
Dio nimale! (par.) *That animal of a God!*
Dio nimel! (par.) *That animal of a God!*
Dio porco! *That pig of a God!*
Dio porc! *That pig of a God!*

Dio prete! *That priest of a God!* In a country with a strong anticlerical tradition the term *prete* is often used pejoratively. *Strozzapreti* ("It strangles priests") is the name of several Italian dishes. According to Robert Di Pietro, this term is derived from the priests' reputation of being big, greedy eaters. Naming a dish *strozzapreti* thus indicates that it is so generous that it would even choke a priest.

Dio sagrasco! (rom.) *That sacrament of a God!* (**Dio sacramento!**) The sacrament referred to is the Eucharist or Christ's body. **Corpo di Cristo!** ("Body of Christ") is a very old Italian blasphemy, and there was no end of trouble in Italy when the Church switched from Latin to the vernacular in its services. Instead of saying *Corpus Christi* in Latin during Mass, priests had to say *Corpo di Cristo*, thus introducing blasphemy into the heart of the liturgy.

Dio sagraschio! (rom.) *That sacrament of a God!*

Dio sagrataccio! (rom.) *That sacrament of a God!*

Dio sagrato! (rom.) *That sacrament of a God!*

Dio sborà! (ven.) *God jacked-off! That jacked-off God!* From *sborar(e)* "to ejaculate."

Dio serpente! (ven.) *That snake of a God!*

Dio sarpente! (ven.) *That snake of a God!*

Dio scanpà! (ven.) *God ran off!*

Dio scapà da lett! (par.) *God escaped from bed!*

Dio scapà da lett senza scarpi! (par.) *God escaped from bed without shoes!* This and the following forms help reduce the blasphemy by their expansion.

Dio scapà da lett senza gambe! (par.) *God escaped from bed without legs!*

Dio scapà da lett in bicicletta! (par.) *God escaped from bed by bicycle!*

Dio sallarga! (rom.) *Expanding God!* Euphemism for **Dio sacramento!**

Dio s'allarga! (rom.) *Expanding God!*
Dio serenella! (rom.) *Cloudless God!* 19th century, military use.
Dio travo! (ven.) *That beam of a God!*
Dio impalato! (tosc.) *That shafted God!*
Dio rospo! (tosc.) *That toad of a God!*
Orco Dio! (ven.) *That pig of a God!* Euphemism for **Porco Dio!**
Orco zio! (ven.) *That pig of a God!* Double euphemism.
Per Dio! *By God!*
Per brio (par.) *By God!* Euphemism.
Par bio! (par.) *By God!* Euphemism.
Pebbio! (rom.) *By God!* Euphemism.
Peddio! (rom.) *By God!* Euphemism.
Peddio sagranne! (rom.) *By holy God!* Euphemism.
Peddio sagraschio! (rom.) *By holy God!* Euphemism.
Peddio de legno! (rom.) *By wooden God!* Euphemism.
Perdio sagrato! (rom.) *By holy God!*
Perdio santo a le bocie! (veron.) *By holy God playing bocce! By holy bowling God!* Blasphemy reduced by expansion.
Pardia! (veron.) *By God!* Euphemism.
Par die! (veron.) *By God!* Euphemism.
Par didedi! (veron.) *By God!* Euphemism.
Pardiu! (cal.) *By God!* Euphemism.
Pardeu! (cal.) *By God!* Euphemism.
Parbeu! (cal.) *By God!* Euphemism.
Pardena! (cal.) *By God!* Euphemism.
Perdena! (cal.) *By God!* Euphemism.
Perdeu! (cal.) *By God!* Euphemism.
Porco Dio! *That pig of a God!*
Porco zio! *That pig of a God!* Euphemism; *zio* means "uncle."
Porki dia! *That pig of a God!* Euphemism. Sometimes *porco* is written with a *k*, just as *cazzo* "prick" is seen written as *kazzo*.
Porco diose! (ven.) *That pig of a God!* Euphemism.

Porco madono! (ven.) *That pig of a Madonna!*
Sacher Dieu! (mil.) *Holy God!* Cf. the French *sacrebleu!* where *bleu* "blue" is a phonetic euphemism for *Dieu* "God." In French, however, *sacre* has retained the original double meaning of the Latin *sacer*: "holy" and "accursed." Thus *sacrebleu!* means "damned God!"
Sangue di Dio! *Blood of God!*
Sangue de Dio! (ven.) *Blood of God!*
Sangue de bio! (rom.) *Blood of God!* Euphemism.
Sango de bio! (par.) *Blood of God!* Euphemism.
Sanguanon de bia! (mil.) *Blood of God!* Euphemism.
Sandiocan! (ven.) *That dog of a holy God!*
Santo Dio! *Holy God!*
Santi dia! (sic.) *Holy God!*
Santu dia! (sic.) *Holy God!*
Vaca dio! (ven.) *That cow of a God! That whore of a God!* — *Vaca* "cow" is one of the most common insults meaning "whore."
Zio porco! (ven.) *That pig of a God!* Euphemism; *zio* "uncle."
Zio cane! (ven.) *That dog of a God!* Euphemism.
Zio can! (ven.) *That dog of a God!* Euphemism.
Zio schitaron! *That chickenshitting God!* — *Schito* is "chicken shit," and *schitarar* means "to defecate," especially in reference to chickens.

How did the Polack get 35 holes in his head?
—*He was trying to learn to eat with a fork.*

Why did 50 whales beach themselves in Mexico?
—*Because they thought it was Guyana.*

Why do KGB agents always go in threes?
—*Because one can read, one can write, and the third keeps an eye on these two intellectuals.*

Japanese Sexual Maledicta

John Solt

The following sample of Japanese "bad words" is translated into English for the first time. Instead of employing R. Aman's method of categorizing maledicta by provenance, I selected them for poetic quality and rounded them out with some musts.

Poetry continues to shape the language as it has through the 1200-year history of Japanese literature. On the whole, Japanese in conversation relate rhythmically and with ambiguous gaps — poetic techniques — rather than through prosy recourse to logical exposition. The vast body of Japanese poetry written with hidden allusions to the past is an example of the vivid manner in which the tradition is kept alive, as is the frequent recourse to proverbs even by laborers.

During the years I lived in Japan (1974-1980), and prodded by our editor, I jotted down colorful words and sayings whenever they caught my attention. Most foreigners believe that Japanese is sparse in maledicta, which is not true. However, they can be quite subtle at times and tend to bypass square-heads conditioned to blunt ravings of the "up yours, shithead, motherfucker" variety.

Japanese maledicta are less direct than those of other countries because subversive language and thought had to be concealed during the time Japan was isolated from the

---

MAY ALL YOUR TEETH FALL OUT, EXCEPT ONE, SO YOU CAN HAVE A TOOTHACHE!

outside world (Edo period, 1600-1868), when the intellectually and financially superior merchants were stratified socially on the bottom rung, below the samurai, farmers, and artisans. Therefore, in order to capture some of the sophistication of the maledicta of old and modern Japan, I have included not only the abusive side of language but also encrypted and symbolic language which alludes to sexuality.

As mentioned above, it is a mere sampling and presented with the hope that others will add to it and compile a more exhaustive list. I would like to thank everyone who suggested them to me, and especially Keiko Kanda for offering her award-winning calligraphy.

豆腐の角に頭をぶつけて死んしまえ

Tofu no kado ni atama o butsukete shinde shimae!
"Go knock your head on a corner of *tofu* and die!" Although spoken in anger, this expression is not very hostile because *tofu* (bean curd) is softer than marshmallow and would cause no damage to a bumped head.

Senzuri 千擦り
"One thousand rubs" : Male masturbation.

Manzuri 万擦り
"Ten thousand rubs" : Masturbation performed by females. *The Hite Report*, in which some women attest to masturbating for up to five hours, confirms that women's genital self-play is more time-consuming than male masturbation.

Niwatori にわとり
"Chicken" : This is a current slang word for a man who prematurely ejaculates, likened to a chicken nervously flapping its wings.

Sōrō 早漏
"Fast leak" : A man who ejaculates prematurely.

朝うらのたたぬ男に金貸すな。
Asamara no tatanu otoko ni kane kasuna.
"Never lend money to a man who doesn't have a hard-on in the morning" : This proverb from the southwestern island of Kyushu has a practical intention at its base; if he doesn't have an erection in the morning, he isn't healthy and will probably die before repaying the money.

Sukebe スケベイ
"Lusty" : Every Japanese is familiar with the saying that the three lustiest groups of "dirty old men" are doctors, teachers, and monks. From an Edo fiction character.

Chikan 痴漢
"Sexual grabber" : As with pinching in Italy, and exacerbated by crowded trains, illegal grabbing of flesh abounds in Japan. A few years ago there was a poster campaign around parks and dark alleys warning of *chikan*, depicted with a wolf's head.

Tsubo arai 壷洗い
"Jug-washing" : Douching. The vagina is seen as an upside-down jug.

おまんこに豚の足を突込んで奥歯が
ガタガタ云わせてやる。

Omanko ni buta no ashi o tsukkonde okuba gata-gata iwasete yaru!
"I'll stick a pig's leg up your cunt until your back-teeth rattle!" : This expression is most frequently uttered by cuckolded men and *yakuza* withdrawing from hard drugs. *Yazuka* are the "Japanese mafia." They often shoot speed and sometimes are jailed for it. If they violate their own code, they can apologize by having a small finger chopped off. They are easily detectable by their large American cars, dark sunglasses, tattoos, and lack of a finger or more.

Omanko おまんこ
"Cunt" : The word *manko* (in dialect, *meko*) is used mostly by men and prostitutes. Other women usually refer to their vulva indirectly as *asoko*, "there." As with countless other nouns in Japanese, an *o-* is prefixed to exalt the object in respect, or to denigrate it ironically.

Chinko ちんこ
"Cock" : Maybe because of its similarity in sound to the baby-talk word for penis, *chin-chin*, "pee-pee, wee-wee", *chinko* is less taboo than *manko*. The English word "penis," mispronounced "pay-ness," is currently used as frequently as its Japanese counterpart, especially by men.

Isoginchaku 磯巾着
"A clam that shrivels" : Euphemism for vulva and round coin purses which, when squeezed, open their slit.

Ippai soba 一杯そば

"One cup noodle" : A noodle-cup fuck. Dehydrated noodles are sold in a styrofoam cup, needing only hot water and a few minutes before they are soft enough to be eaten. Over the last ten years, school boys have developed the practice of cutting out the styrofoam bottom and filling the cup with lukewarm water. As the noodles soften, the penis is inserted and "goes at it."

随喜の涙を流す
Zuiki no namida o nagasu

"To let flow tears of zuiki" : The Shogun employed various methods to control the populace during the centuries of seclusion: boats large enough to sail to foreign lands were forbidden to be built; people caught trying to enter or exit Japan (except accredited foreigners) were killed; barriers were set up between provinces, and one needed reasons and papers to travel; provincial lords (*daimyō*) were kept hostage in Edo (Tokyo) for long periods of time to insure their allegiance. When arriving in the capital, the *daimyō* offered the Shogun famous products of their region. The *daimyō* from the province of Higo (present-day Kumamoto) brought *higo-zuiki*, "cock-rings" and dildos made from the pliant *zuiki* plant, which secretes an itch-causing juice. A mild Spanish fly, the *zuiki* is reputed to have caused the Shogun's numerous concubines to flow orgasmic tears of joy. The expression is innocently used in the sense of "happy as a lark," because few who utter it are aware of the derivation. In these days of rabbit-headed, three-pronged, battery-operated vibrators and other paraphernalia available in Japanese porn shops (*otona no omochaya*, lit. 'adult toys shop'), the *higo-zuiki* seem relatively tame stimuli.

Giri-man 義理さん

"Obligation-cunt" : A wife allowing herself to be fucked on an off-night. Women were traditionally expected to take care of their husband's sexual needs even when their own were not aroused. There is no corresponding term of "obligation-cock."

Shakuhachi 尺八

"Bamboo flute" : The common word for fellatio. On the other hand, or mouth, the word for cunnilingus is *hamōnika*, "harmonica," derived from this Western musical instrument that produces pleasant sounds when tongue and lips are moved correctly.

Etchi エッチ

"Pervert" : From the pronunciation of the letter *h*, the first letter in romanized script of *hentai*, "pervert." The idea of using the abbreviated Roman letter of a transcribed Japanese word gives this expression a certain uniqueness, helping its spread.

Kintama 金玉

"Golden balls" : Commonly used by men to refer to their testicles. According to the well-known feminist poet in Tokyo, Sachiko Yoshihara, "No woman would call them golden or silver, just balls."

The fingers of an open hand (thumb facing up). Each finger represents the angle of a man's erect penis during a decade of his life: during his 20s, 30s, etc.

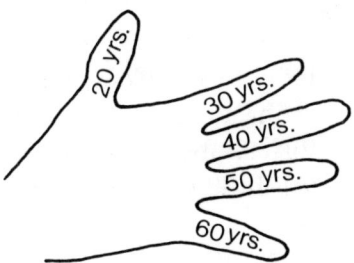

Nozoki のぞき

"Peeping Tom": The great lovers, from the earliest Japanese novels of one thousand years ago to the present, have all been avid peepers. Partly because of the non-fortification of ancient Japanese architecture and partly because peeping is not considered a sin (as defined by the Christian West), voyeurism has been viewed favorably—or at least tolerated—as only slightly naughty. In fact, the latest sex craze budding in Tokyo (summer 1982) is peeping-tom parlors (*nozokiba*). The peeper enters a closet-size room containing a chair, a box of tissues, and a tiny crevice to gaze through. In the dim light of the main room a lady makes herself up, surrounded by about 20 small closets. A recording informs the customers that she cannot see those peeping on her. The light increases, and she dances around, presses her body against the various slots, and performs *manzuri* ("10,000 rubs") on the carpet, accompanied by the recorded sounds of a female moaning orgasmically.

一寸八分の観音様

Issun hachibu no kannon-sama

"A *kannon* of 1 *sun* 8 *bu* measurement": Kannon (goddess of mercy) was the Indian Bodhisattva (helper of Buddha) with moustache who was considered male or asexual in China, but was thought of as asexual or female in Japan. This sex change performed on Kannon by Japanese culture through centuries, as well as the native Shinto religious belief that the highest deity, the sun (*amaterasu*), is a woman, have led psychological anthropologists to claim that Japan is a female (mother) oriented society. One *sun*, an archaic measurement, is less than one inch, and 10 *bu* equal one *sun*. In Edo slang, this miniature goddess, about 1½ inches high, represented the clitoris in size, shape, and concept. It specifically refers to the image housed at Asakusa Temple.

The author appreciates R. Aman's help with this article.

Yugoslavia, Here I Come

Reinhold Aman

In my selfless dedication to introduce you to foreign tongues and to provide you with useful and socially redeeming knowledge, I have been searching every conceivable verbal avenue. Undaunted, I have been reading, and shuddering at, the thinly veiled pornography oozing even from allegedly clean books, of which our bookstores and libraries are full.

Yes, even books owned by bigots or kept in libraries, including those designated by the librarians for juvenile consumption, are chock-full of blatant sexuality — *if you can spot it*. Scenes of gross lascivity are cleverly dispersed throughout the pages of any "clean" book; most of them will escape the untrained reader who merely looks for a "cunt" here and a "fuck" there, as used by the so-called great novelists of our times to jerk up book sales. But that is not my concern today; I am talking about the far greater obscenity found in allegedly harmless books that contain no "four-letter words" but which are so filthy that they would arouse even a lobotomized university administrator.

The sixteen years I have been spending in the linguistic research of "bad words" are paying off. Now I can see even through the ruses of publishers of foreign-language guides. Take, for example, the Berlitz *Serbo-Croatian for Travellers* (Lausanne, 1973). Supposedly a "clean" phrase-book for Mr. and Mrs. Average Traveler—who would retch if they knew what smut is in their little verbal helpers—this booklet contains such raunchy stuff that I was forced to take several icy-cold showers while reading it—and that *before* I reached the chapter "Doctor." Don't blame *me* for any unhealthy sexual arousals you might experience while reading the following pages: I am just reporting *verbatim* from that book, not adding one *háček*.

One should also refrain from accusing the Yugoslavs of being lewd. They can't help it. The same kind of smutty material can be found in practically any language phrase-book. I just chanced upon Serbo-Croatian, having been introduced recently to a lady who speaks this tongue, amongst others. Naturally, cunning linguist that I am, I acquired that little language guide to be able to employ this tongue during our next meeting.

Following below are four scenes constructed from the most blatant erotic words & phrases listed in that Berlitz phrasebook. In addition to demonstrating the hidden, four-letter-word-less porno of allegedly clean books, the phrases—if memorized properly—will also come in handy when traveling in Yugoslavia. Armed with such useful expressions (including several alternative replies), you should be able to handle decently whatever might arise. *Gute Fahrt!*

SCENE 1

HE: *Dobar dan. Kako ste?* — Good afternoon. How are you?
SHE: *Milo mi je da sam Vas upoznao.* — I'm very pleased to meet you.
HE: *Molim Vas skinite se.* — Please undress.
SHE: *Odlazite!* — Go away!
HE: *Lezite!* — Lie down!
SHE: *Prestanite ili ću vikati!* — Stop or I'll scream!
HE: *Da li je ovo prvi put da ste to dobili?* — Is this the first time you've had this?
SHE: *Da.* — Yes.
HE: *Želeo bih to što pre.* — I'd like it as soon as possible.
SHE: *Kako?* — How?
HE: *Guraj i vuci!* — Push and pull!
SHE: *Hvala Vam.* — Thank you.
HE: *Guraj!* — Push!
SHE: *Ne suviše nazad.* — Not too far back.
HE: *Vuci!* — Pull!
SHE: *Hoćete li doći? Samo trenutak??* — Are you coming? Just a minute??
HE: *Nisam primetio da tako brzo vozim....* — I didn't realize my speed....
SHE: *Ne želim da ga izvadim!* — I don't want it extracted (pulled out)!
HE: *Hoćete li mi, molim Vas, reći kad treba da sidjem?* — Will you tell me when to get off?

SHE: *Rado bih došla.* — I'd love to come.
HE: *Nadam se da možete doći.* — I do hope you can come.
SHE: *To je vrlo ljubazno od Vas.* — That's very kind of you.
HE: *Doći ćemo opet.* — We'll come again some time.
SHE: *Hvala, bilo je krasno!* — Thanks, it was a fabulous time!
HE: *Sigurno ćemo se jedanput opet sresti. Zbogom. Ja se zovem Rasputin.* — I'm sure we'll run into each other again some time. Good-bye. My name is Rasputin.

SCENE 2

HE: *Dobro veče! Želim pumperice i sekiru.* — Good evening! I'd like a pair of knickers and an axe.
SHE: *Slobodno. Ulaz slobodan.* — Come in. Entrance free.
HE: *Inekciju ili oralno?* — Injection or oral?
SHE: *Oralno. Ja imam hemoroide.* — Oral. I've got hemorrhoids.
HE: *Otvorite usta.* — Open your mouth.
SHE: *Ja ne razumem.* — I don't understand.
HE: *Otvorite usta!* — Open your mouth!
SHE: *Dobro! To je baš što mi treba.* — Fine! That's just what I want.
HE: *To je krasno / neodoljivo / čudno!* — It's magnificent / overwhelming / strange!
SHE: *Dajte mi to molim Vas!* — Give it to me, please!
HE: *Želim biti unutra / gore / dole.* — I want to be inside / on top / down.
SHE: *Radije bih nešto niže. Želim utikač za ovo.* — I'd rather have something lower down. I want a plug for this.
HE: *Da li Vam odgovara?* — Does it fit?
SHE: *Ne odgorovara mi. Suviše je kratko.* — It doesn't fit. It is too short.
HE: *Možete li me izmeriti?* — Could you measure me?
SHE: *Suviše je malena. Ne, to uopšte ne odgovara. Imate li nešto veće?* — It's too small. No, that won't do at all. Have you anything bigger?
HE: *Moja mera je 15,24 cm!* — My size is 6 inches!
SHE: *Želim jedan veliki. Odlazite!* — I'd like a large one. Go away!
HE (to himself): *Ružna je! Čuvaj se psa!!* — She is ugly! Beware of the dog!!

SCENE 3

HE: *Dobro veče. Kako ste?* — Good evening. How are you?
SHE: *Vruće!* — Hot!
HE: *Molim Vas skinite gaćice.* — Please remove your underpants.
SHE: *Da.* — Yes.
HE: *Da li ste slobodni večeras?* — Are you free this evening?
SHE: *Ne.* — No.
HE: *Koliko staje?* — How much is that?
SHE: *100 dinara.* — Hundred dinars.
HE: *To je suviše skupo. Zar nemate ništa jeftinije?* — That's too expensive. Haven't you anything cheaper?
SHE: *Ne. Ne diraj! Imao sam srčani napad.* — No. Don't touch! I had a heart attack.
HE: *Ja imam prst!* — I've got a finger!
SHE: *I imam zatvor! Ulaz zabranjen!* — And I'm constipated! No entry!
HE: *Možete li mi poneti krastavac / jegulja / banana / kokosov orah?* — Can you help me with my cucumber / eel / banana / coconuts?
SHE: *Stavite ih ovde, molim Vas.* — Put them down here, please.
HE: *Hvala Vam.* — Thank you.
SHE: *Molim Vas lezite ovde.* — Please lie down over here.
HE: *Kako želite vaše meso?* — How do you like your meat?
SHE: *Filovano!* — Stuffed!
HE: *Možete li pogledati otuk?* — Could you have a look at this swelling?
SHE: *Samo trenutak. Videću da li mogu da je nadjem.* — Just a minute. I'll see if I can find it.
HE: *Požurite!* — Hurry up!
SHE: *Kako se ovo zove?* — What do you call this?
HE: *Glava / kost / osovina / pumpa uštrcavanja / viršle. Otvorite usta!* — Head / bone / shaft / injection pump / hot dog. Open your mouth!
SHE: *Ne, to ne mogu da jedem. To je grozno / ružno / strašno!* — No, I can't eat this. It's hideous / ugly / awful!
HE: *Molim!* — Please!

SHE: *Ne. Ja imam ukočen vrat.* — No. I've got a stiff neck.
HE: *Molim!* — Please!
SHE: *Ne! Ja imam upala jezik!* — No! I have an inflammation of the tongue!
HE: *Molim!!* — Please!!
SHE: *Ne, ne! Ja imam gušobolju!* — No, no! I've got a sore throat!
HE: *Molim Vas!!* — I beg you!!
SHE: *Ne! Muka mi je i slomila sam protezu!* — No! I feel nauseated and I have this broken denture!
HE: *Dajte mi to molim Vas!* — Give it to me, pleeeeeze!
SHE: *Ne, danas nije. Crvena zastava je dignuta.* — No, not today. The red flag is up.

SCENE 4

HE: *Dobro jutro! Možete li mi pokazati tvoje grudi?* — Good morning! Can you show me your breast?
SHE: *Zašto?* — Why?
HE: *Rado bih došao!* — I'd love to come!
SHE: *Možete li pogledati bedro / paštetu dole?* — Could you have a look at this thigh / pie below?
HE: *Kad?* — When?
SHE: *Sada! Požurite! Hitno je!* — Now! Hurry up! It's urgent!
HE: *Želim ga jedanput, dva puta, tri puta!* — I want it once, twice, three times!
SHE: *Želim ga u jutro, u toku dana, posle podne, u veče i noću!!* — I want it in the morning, during the day, in the afternoon, in the evening, and at night!!
HE: *Suviše je tesno!* — It's too tight!
SHE: *Možete li to uraditi sada?* — Can you do it now?
HE: *Ne. Ja mislim da nešto nije u redu sa sistemom podmazivanja.* — No. I think there's something wrong with the lubrication system.
SHE: *Ne!* — No!
HE: *Da! To je bučno / curi / dotrajalo / lupa / pregrejavanje / spada / suvo / vibrira / zaglavljeno!* — Yes! It's noisy / leaking / worn / knocking / overheating / slipping / dry / vibrating / stuck!

SHE: *Vi ste premoreni. Potreban Vam je mir.* — You're overtired. You need a rest.
HE: *Da. Nadamo se da ćemo opet doći! Zbogom.* — Yes. We hope to come again some day! Good-bye.

Airborn(e) Bullshit

E. A. "Jerry" Jerome

One stormy night, when visibilities and ceilings were pushing minimums, aircraft flights were being stacked up all over the terminal areas. The inordinate delays and the incessant holding patterns were starting to unnerve both pilots and ground controllers. A few pilots started to hound Air Traffic Control for immediate descent and approach clearances. One intrepid but harassed controller had his fill, and snarled into the microphone on a frequency heard by most of the impatient crews, "I'll get you guys down as soon as I can. We are doing the best we know how."

A slight silence, and then an unidentified voice loudly uttered a caustic but effective vulgarism, "**Bullshit!**"

The controller took offense at the language and barked officiously, "Attention all flights! Who said that!?"

After a dramatic pause, one by one, the pious denials came in with standard but bizarre phraseology:

> "United 345: Negative on the bullshit."
> "American 52: Negative on the bullshit."
> "Northwest 302: Negative on the bullshit."
> "Continental 602: Negative on the bullshit."
> "Delta 410: Negative on the bullshit."
> "JAL 002: Negative on the bullshit."

Teenage Jokesters and Riddlers
A Profile in Parody

Brigitta Geltrich–Ludgate

This article is dedicated to Spencer Ludgate and his many friends, without whose cooperation this research would not have been possible.

INTRODUCTION

Teenagers incorporate satire in jokes and riddles to direct aggression toward peers, thereby protecting themselves from becoming that what the joke or riddle relates; toward themselves, to protect personal behavioral or physiological discrepancies from being ridiculed by peers; and toward authority figures, therewith attempting to settle in their own way the authority conflict.

In order to analyze jokes and riddles told by children, I conducted a preliminary search through archives and the literature on children's jokes and riddles. The search revealed little analytic research. Scholars in the past were satisfied with compiling the data. Studies into content and functions of children's jokes and riddles, particularly satirical content, are sparce and have only recently accelerated, for instance with such works as John Holmes McDowell's *Children's Riddling* (1979) or Sandra McCosh's *Children's Humour* (1980).

A further search revealed that often no distinctions were made between the type of joke and riddle told by children and those told by adults about children. Even though the borderline between these two types appears at times hazy,

---

What do you get when you cross a Cabbage Patch doll with the Pillsbury doughboy?
— *An ugly, squatty broad with a yeast infection.*

it nonetheless exists. Adults tend to tell jokes and riddles about children in such a way as if they were originated by children. The chance that children will actually originate/create a joke or riddle is slim. Children observe and experiment with material heard from older peers and adults, and then will readapt the material to their current needs and trends.

To determine what types of jokes and riddles children relate, whether they use already-heard material to create their own jokes and riddles, I empirically studied a group of Los Angeles junior-high teenagers (ages 13 through 15) over a three-year period and interviewed those of them who felt comfortable to be interviewed. The data collected from these informants are one-sided, in that all the informants were boys and all enrolled in a gifted program at the Los Angeles Unified School District. They felt that they were wittier and more intelligent than other teenagers on the school and playground.

The present study is part of a more extensive study currently in progress, in which I compare jokes and riddles of American children with the jokes and riddles of German children. The two genres are treated here as related, due to their inherent relationship; that is, riddles pose questions, and jokes answer questions (Bausinger, 1968). The relationship is even further intensified in that *within* jokes often new riddles are posed and that jokes often appear in riddle form.

RIDDLES AND JOKES

The greats of antiquity—Homer, Hesiod, Pindar, and others—already knew the riddle. So did the authors of the *Rig-Veda* approximately 3,000 years ago and the members of ancient Jewish and Arabian traditions. Unlike the riddle of antiquity which was the property of adults, the riddle of today is much relegated to being the property of children (Coffin & Cohen, 1974). Coffin and Cohen claim that the appeal of a riddle to the well-educated is limited. I do not fully concur with this contention, because my research revealed that the older child tells a more sophisticated riddle or joke than the younger child. Also, the so-called "thinking" or "mathematical" riddles which sporadically appear on American university campuses require considerable thought before they can be solved. Like mathematical equations, the words uttered in the riddle have to be thoroughly analyzed before one comes to the definitive answer. These "thinking" riddles, in a somewhat less sophisticated form, already exist on the junior-high playground:

(1) How are things on Jupiter lately?
Heavy, heavy.
(Personal collection, Los Angeles, Grade 9, 1980)

(2) How are things on Pluto?
Cool, baby, cool.
(Personal collection, Los Angeles, Grade 9, 1980)

To answer these questions, children must be familiar with the density and atmosphere of the planetary system.

"Thinking" riddles are not told by younger children. Just as they baffle the teenager's peers, they baffle adult listeners. Riddles and jokes belong to all ages with certain types of riddles and jokes more popular at a specific age level than others. However, not everybody tells riddles and jokes. It takes certain skills to tell them effectively. Here again a difference between the adult and child jokester and riddler can be observed. Skilled adult riddlers and jokesters pay closer attention to coherency, proper placing of punch lines, and evocation of laughter at the right place. Children, on the other hand, notoriously ignore the point, or often retell imperfectly a riddle or joke previously heard. They complicate their jokes, and the milieu out of which children create their jokes and riddles vary from the milieu of adults. A riddle or joke posed by children is at times not understood by adults, and that what appears funny to children many times evades stimulating the humor nerve of adults.

The Riddle. A riddle is a question which can be asked by anyone at any age level. Foremost in posing riddles, according to André Jolles (1929), is the relationship that exists between the poser and the posee. The poser has knowledge of the riddle, the posee must prove him/herself equal in wit or intelligence to the poser by correctly answering it. At this point, the riddle—particularly the one containing satirical and ridiculing elements—becomes of importance in the socialization process of children on the play territory. Primary socializers of children are peers, who belong to ingroups and outgroups. In order to be accepted to a play territory and its dominant (in)group, a child cannot afford to be ridiculed (Ludgate, 1980b).* He/she also cannot afford to appear academically less well equipped than the members of the ingroup, who choose to accept or reject children to the play territory often according to the wit/intelligence, as well as the popularity, of the outsider. By posing riddles with answers known only to the initiates of the ingroup to a child new on the play territory or unpopular, the poser deters the unwanted or unpopular child from joining the group or from participating in the activities of telling jokes and riddles. This is particularly so with riddles used in counting-out rhymes, where the answer is often concealed within the rhyme, a specific language, or in an ingroup code. From the outset, an unwanted or unpopular child will not be able to solve the riddle due to unfamiliarity with the specific language or code.

Children also tell riddles and jokes for the purpose of competition, where one child attempts to outriddle or outjoke the other. This competitive confrontation starts out in jest, but soon grows into an aggressive combat, where

---
*See *Geltrich-Ludgate* for references to *Ludgate*.

each child is determined to outriddle or outjoke the other. In this aggressive combat, the coherency of the individual genres usually suffers, and riddles and jokes turn into nonsensical utterances.

Interestingly, the teenagers interviewed claimed that on the whole they do not tell riddles, unless they allude to some taboo or a joke is contained in the riddle:

(3) Why did Humpty Dumpty have a great fall?
To make up for his rotten summer.
(From the private publication, *The Creative with Words Club*, September/October 1978, p. 8; Informant Robert Tejada, Age 14)

Of great popularity is the riddle which anticipates an obscene answer but comes to a perfectly acceptable conclusion:

(4) What does a man do standing up, a woman sitting down, and a dog on three legs?
Shake hands.
(Personal collection, Los Angeles, Grade 9, 1979; also from "The Benny Hill Show")

(5) What does a cow have four of and a woman only two?
Legs.
(Personal collection, Los Angeles, Grade 9, 1979; probably from "The Benny Hill Show")

(6) What does the man have in his trousers that is on the pool table?
Pockets.
(Personal collection, Los Angeles, Grade 9, 1979; from "The Benny Hill Show")

The Joke. The joke is an answer to a riddle. That does not exclude that there are many jokes in riddle form. A joke contains a punch line which carries humor and evokes laughter. Children enjoy incorporating taboo terms into this punch line:

(7) Three men were in a room at a Catholic school, telling dirty jokes. In walks a nun and the three tried to discourage her from staying. First one gets up and says:
   "I was two weeks old when my parents got married."
The nun does not respond. Second one gets up and says:
   "I was a year old when my parents got married."
The nun does not respond. Third one gets up and says:
   "That's nothing. I still don't know who my father is."
That moment the nun says: "Would any of you three bastards please pass me the Bible?"
(Personal collection, Los Angeles, Grade 9, 1979)

By telling jokes flavored with satirical, ridiculing, and taboo elements, children vent hostility and direct aggression toward peers (usually not present), toward themselves, authority figures, and others. In directing aggressive jokes toward others, children protect themselves from becoming that what the joke relates, and in directing jokes toward themselves, they protect themselves from a behavioral or physiological discrepancy being found out by peers, who could then direct their aggression toward them. In directing aggressive behavior toward authority figures, children try to settle in their own way the authority conflict.

DATA ANALYSIS

The group of junior-high teenagers, who were studied for this paper, claimed that they tell impromptu jokes and riddles, personally created to amuse others (outsiders) as well as themselves (insiders). Caution should be taken with this claim on two accounts: first, teenagers may well tell impromptu jokes, but in doing so they use what they have heard before and rearrange it to adapt it to their own situation; second, teenagers go beyond telling riddles and jokes to amuse outsiders and insiders; they also use them as means to convey aggressive behavior.

In further probing the informants, they admitted that they do retell adult jokes, which are seldom those overheard from parents and other family members, but those from situation comedies and television and from entertainers. Prime comedy shows which exude great influence on teenage jokesters are "Fridays," "Saturday Night Live," and "Make me Laugh." Prime idols of the joke-telling entertainment world are such veterans as Bob Hope, Don Rickles, and of more recent vintage, Robin Williams ("Mork from Ork") along with the British television star Benny Hill and the characters of "Monty Python's Flying Circus."

The following analysis will primarily center on the joke, or on the joke that exists in riddle form, because the teenagers interviewed informed that they spent more time on telling jokes and little or none at all on posing riddles.

Jokes Directed Against Peers

The two most popular types of the play territory jokes directed at peers are the "cutting low" and the "sex" joke. Within the group they are told in jest. The purpose of telling these jokes was to express the teenagers' clever execution of wit and verbal skill, while at the same time — often without the teenagers' awareness — to release desires and hostilities that are normally suppressed (Wolfenstein, 1954). Outsiders, particularly those who were less academically gifted, were downgraded:

(8) Steven Motts is so stupid, it takes him an hour to cook minute rice.
(Personal collection, Los Angeles, Grade 8, 1979)

Jokes directed against members of the opposite sex were aggressive and at the same time served as a means to steady the ambivalence of hostility felt toward the opposite sex and being drawn toward it. The informants had singled out one girl, who was behind her age in physical development, and made her the target of their ridicule and jokes. For this study she has been renamed "Bonny" and the jokes about her to "Bonny jokes":

> (9) Bonny's chest was [rented] by an architectural firm to use as a straightedge. She got fired and then worked for a construction firm as a mold for brick walls.
> (Personal collection, Los Angeles, Grade 9, 1979)

The informants were no less aware of their own sex's under- or overdevelopment and told jokes about it without reservation:

> (10) There's a man. He says he has the longest dick in the world. He gets a job at a railroad workshop. The foreman says *he* has the longest dick in the world. They have an argument, but they become good friends. One day, they were going to cross the Golden Gate Bridge. They decide to take a pee. So they go to take a piss over the bridge. One says, "Brrr, that water is cold!" The other says, "Yeah, and deep, too."
> (Personal collection, Los Angeles, Grade 8, 1979)

Great humor presented the teenagers' zippers, particularly their open position:

> (11) Are you modest?
> *Yes, I am.*
> Your zipper ain't.
> (Personal collection, Los Angeles, Grade 9, 1980)

> (12) Did the president die today?
> *No.*
> Then how come your fly is at half mast?
> (Personal collection, Los Angeles, Grade 9, 1980)

Jokes incorporating taboo terminology are popular if the taboo centers on sex terminology. The teenagers' general sex jokes are extremely bawdy, yet cleverly constructed by playing with words:

> (13) What do you call a depressed slut-fucker?
> *A mopey dick.*
> (Personal collection, Los Angeles, Grade 9, 1980)

Scatological jokes and riddles at the teenage level no longer enjoy as much popularity as they did at an earlier age level. There are a few remnants, mostly because of their nature to readily rhyme with anal and fecal terms:

(14) Uranus!
Fred: What about my anus?
(Personal collection, Los Angeles, Grade 8, 1979)

(15) Bob gives order to dog: "Sit!"
Dog obeys.
Bob: "Sit, I said, not shit!"
(Personal collection, Los Angeles, Grade 8, 1979; joke appeared in a *Playboy* cartoon of the mid-1970s)

Jokes Directed Against Oneself

Survival on the play or school territory hinges on becoming an insider of the group. Being accepted by the group, however, is not lasting. Children, therefore, must be cautious not to become subject to ridicule.

Personal shortcomings. To remain popular, children often hide their own shortcomings behind a joke, which they direct toward themselves, in order to beat the other child at the chance of making fun of the shortcoming. One of the informants, for instance, was afflicted with a dermatological problem; that is, he had a severe case of dandruff and along with it stringy hair. To ward off jokes made about his condition by peers and thus having his popularity within the group jeopardized, the teenager devised a number of hair and dandruff jokes, for example:

(16) My lice are so civilized they ride fleas. They live in buildings made of flakes of dandruff.
(Personal collection, Los Angeles, Grade 8, 1979)

It is interesting to note that this joke makes fun of both of the teenager's problems, and could also be considered a revolt against an overly hygenic preoccupation of

American households and the school system, namely the nightly ritual of washing one's hair.

Legitimacy of birth is also a factor which causes children to direct jokes against themselves. The question of legitimacy is no longer a major cause for ridicule as in the past. Yet, jokes are nonetheless made about the origin of individuals as was already evidenced in (7) above. If remarks about illegitimacy are made, they are generally made by the individual him/herself who is in doubt about his/her legitimacy. A deep-seated fear of being found out illegitimate must still exist, no matter how lightly the informants treated this subject.

Jokes About Authority Figures and Others. Authority figures and others are not all equally subject to ridicule in teenage jokes.

Those least subject to ridicule are the parents and religion. First, the informants unanimously denied making jokes about parents, claiming that they openly complain about their parents among the group and do not have to vent their aggression through a joke. Delight is nonetheless expressed when attacking the norms established by parents. One such norm is cleanliness:

(17) *Son*: I got a shock when I went to my room today.
Mom: Why?
Son: It was all cleaned up.
(Personal collection, Los Angeles, Grade 8, 1978/79)

Second, the informants also did not make religious jokes, possibly because in the American education system religion is not a mandatory subject, and therefore is not ridiculed like other school subjects. Also, not all children — particularly not the teenagers involved in this study — go to Sunday school or other religious classes for confirmation of faith. The interviewees were a religiously integrated group, holding Greek Orthodox, Roman Catholic, Anglo-

Catholic, Baptist, Mormon, and Jewish faiths. There was little interest expressed in singling out one religion and making jokes about it. This does not exclude American children, in general, from making religious jokes. From personal recollection of the late 1950s and early 1960s, religious jokes were made to varying degrees:

(18)   *Son*: Is it true that we are made of dust and will go to dust?
Mom: That is what the Bible tells us.
Son: Okay, Mom, then somebody under my bed is either coming or going.

Those most subject to ridicule are the school and anything associated with it: teachers, subjects, norms, school food, etc. The school is an alien institution, and the teacher is a representative of such an alien institution which offers little affection and often little understanding to children. Children, thus, aggressively strike back with verbal attacks.

1. Teachers: Anything about the teacher—such as his/her name, occupation, personal behavior, looks, and characteristics—is being mercilessly ridiculed. The ridicule itself is considered a joke. In ridiculing a teacher's occupation as electronic's shop teacher, for instance, the teenagers ridiculed his name as well as his physical appearance by changing the name to "Electrode-head" (Ludgate, 1980a). The mere mentioning of "Electrode-head" evoked a salvo of laughter among the teenagers. On a similar basis, another teacher was ridiculed for wearing a wig. It was the teenagers' greatest challenge to retrieve the wig from the teacher, while she was wearing it. Again the mere simulation of the act of retrieving the wig—mostly behind the teacher's back—resulted in laughter.

2. Subjects are to some extent ridiculed because children feel forced to take them. It should be noted, however, that the following riddle/joke was posed by an informant who liked the subject and felt that he used wit and intelligence in posing it:

(19) French is a very deadly language.
How come?
They have grave accents.
(Personal collection, Los Angeles, Grade 9, 1979/80; this riddle/joke was poorly told: *very deadly:dead, French:they*)

3. Norms: The norm of having to cover textbooks with an appropriate cover and the negligence thereof resulting in a *U* (unsatisfactory) grade on the report card is subject to aggressive revolt. Garbage bags as textbook wrappers appeared to be the most appropriate cover for the teenagers:

(20) *Son*: I believe in the garbage-bag theory.
Mom: What do you mean?
Son: Everything eventually will go into the garbage bag. So why should school textbooks wait?
(Personal collection, Los Angeles, Grade 9, 1979/1980)

4. School Food: The school-food joke carries sarcastic overtones and could equally well be a quip or a taunt. It indicates the ever-present poor-food situation in American schools. The school-food joke attacks directly the food and at times indirectly peers of different ethnic backgrounds:

(21) When the school wants hamburger, it sticks a pair of buns under a pig's nose and asks him to sneeze.
(Personal collection, Los Angeles, Grade 7, 1978)

(22) The school wieners are what they call them.
(Personal collection, Los Angeles, Grade 7, 1978)

(23) The school's orange juice is a coward.
(Personal collection, Los Angeles, Grade 7, 1978)

(24) What is the definition of chocolate milk and white milk?
Nigger milk and honkey milk.
(Personal collection, Los Angeles, Grade 8, 1979)

(25) What is orange juice besides Chinese milk?
Pasturized urine.
(Personal collection, Los Angeles, Grade 7, 1978)

CONCLUSION

The primary reason for telling jokes and riddles among teenagers, according to the teenagers themselves, is not so much a question of aggressively attacking someone as it is a social activity that evokes laughter among the ingroup. It was interesting that within the ingroup one joke after another was told at times until the teenagers could no longer think of a joke. In such joke-telling sessions even a whole batch of bad jokes was tolerated, because the teenagers felt that a bad joke could possibly stimulate them into coming up with a good joke. The informants prided themselves on their wit, in being good jokesters and able to recognize a good joke in the answer of a riddle. They did not feel that intelligence was important, even though they attacked academically less well-equipped peers.

Good jokes and riddles are received with laughter. Not-so-good jokes and bad jokes are received with a repertoire of shouts: "Boo, stale, moldy, bad joke, sucks, stinks!" The response to such a salvo of boos by an insider is generally, "I'm only human." Of note is that with such an expressive repertoire of critical shouts the teenagers were also able to direct aggression toward others in that they launched their salvo of boos even against a good joke if the teller was an unpopular or unwanted individual. The unfortunate individual responded by not participating any further in the ingroup's activity of telling jokes and riddles. The individual thus complied to the ingroup's wish, which was indirectly expressed in the booing in one instance, and in aggressive jokes and riddles in other instances.

REFERENCES

Bausinger, Hermann. *Formen der "Volkspoesie."* Berlin: Erich Schmidt. 1968.

Coffin, Tristram Potter and Hennig Cohen (eds.). *Folklore: From the Working Folk of America.* Garden City, NY: Anchor Books, 1974.

Creative with Words Club. Brigitta Ludgate (ed.). September/October 1978. Los Angeles: Creative with Words Publications, 1978.

Geltrich-Ludgate, Brigitta. "Name Ridiculing, Changing Names, and Playing with Names among Children of the American Southwest." *Southwest Folklore* 4, nos. 3-4 (1980), 72-83.

———. "The Extended Social Functions in Jumping-Rope, Counting-Out, and Autograph-Album Rhymes." Paper presented at the Southern California Academy of Sciences Annual Meeting, May 3, 1980, Long Beach, California.

Hain, Matilda. *Rätsel.* Stuttgart: J.B. Metzler, 1966.

Jolles, André. *Einfache Formen: Legende / Sage / Mythe / Rätsel/ Spruch / Kasus / Memorabile / Märchen / Witz.* Halle, 1929; rpt. Darmstadt, 1958.

McCosh, Sandra. *Children's Humour: A Joke for Every Occasion.* With an Introduction by G. Legman. London: Granada, 1979 (1980).

McDowell, John Holmes. *Children's Riddling.* Bloomington: Indiana University Press, 1979.

Röhrich, Lutz. *Der Witz: Figuren, Formen, Funktionen.* Stuttgart: J.B. Metzler, 1977.

Wolfenstein, Martha. *Children's Humor: A Psychological Analysis.* Glencoe, Illinois: Free Press, 1954. Reissued by Indiana University Press, 1978.

▲ **Breaking Wind Saves Heat.** Headline above an article recommending the planting of wind-breaks around one's house. (*Massachusetts Farm Bulletin,* issue 114 [12 Oct. 1980], p. 8)

▲ Watch your spoonerisms: **E. Elmo Pfudpucker's** (name of a Disco Restaurant in Waukesha, Wisconsin) and **Thaddeus Thudpucker** (name of a Tavern in Las Vegas, Nevada)

▲ The Al-Nasr Automatic Laundry, somewhere in Saudi Arabia, has an English-and-Arabic laundry list. Among the items you can have cleaned are: *Long dress Coulor, Red Kerchief, Suii, Woolen Police Suit, Woollen Planket, Home Rope, Carpest, Colerd Trouser* and **Lady Shit.** (Bob B:, Arabia, 1980)

Academic Graffiti

Weston La Barre

The following graffiti were collected at Drew University, Madison, New Jersey, and date from the 1960 decade:

God is dead. But don't worry; Mary is pregnant again.
    Not *again*! I thought she'd learned. She does it well.
    As Queen of Heaven, where does she stand on birth control?
Against it. A pill a day keeps the messiah away.

Lie down, I think I love you.

Kill all violent people!

When in doubt, worry.

Eunuchs of America unite! You have nothing to lose.

Use erogenous zone numbers.

Reality is a cr$\overset{o}{y}$tch.

Jesus is the answer.
    What is the question?

My mother made me a homosexual.
    If I buy the wool, will she make me one too?

Othello is a bigot.

God is alive and well in Argentina, he just doesn't want to get involved.
    That's right; he doesn't want to get double-crossed.

Hector was a drag.

Chiquita is hooked on bananas.

Dr. Spock wears rubber pants.

God is alive (Billy Graham).   Who is Billy Graham? (God).

Czechoslovakia: love it or leave it.
Impudent snobs, arise!
Accidents cause people.
Drive carefully. Dr. Barnard is waiting for you.
I'd rather fight than swish.
Nobody gets out of life alive.
You're dead right.
This is a grave topic.

* * *

Other graffiti recently collected at The University of North Carolina (Chapel Hill) include:

Free the DC-10!

"Balls," said the queen. "If I had them I'd be king."

Cocaine is like a good joke. You can't wait for the next line.

It's not the length of the wand, but the finesse of the magician that puts the rabbit in the hat.

10% of the people at UNC have hemorrhoids.
The other 90% are perfect assholes.

Carolina could not even get an invitation to the Toilet Bowl.

What do the alligators in Florida have on their chests?
—*Pictures of little Jews.*

What's mass confusion?
—*Father's Day in Oakland.*

What do the flamingos in Florida have on their lawns?
—*Little pink cement Italians.*

Sigma Epsilon XI
Sex in the Typical University Classroom

Don L.F. Nilsen

If you are wondering where to find sex in the typical American university, you need only look as far as the classroom desks. There you will find it in all its lurid detail, carved neatly into the woodwork. For the past three years now my university students and I have been reading our desks as well as our texts. And we have collected an amazingly large and diverse sample of creative graffiti. We were expecting sex to be one of the important preoccupations, but we did not realize the extent of its significance until we counted and found that approximately one out of every five pieces of graffiti related in some way to sex.

Most of what we have collected is going into a textbook showing how creativity works in language, but that which is sex-related is so entertaining that we were afraid people would concentrate on the content instead of the language processes. Besides with censors being what they are, a textbook containing such choice tidbits would probably never make it into the classroom. But believing in what the National Council of Teachers of English calls, "The student's right to his own language," we did not want to see all of this creativity disappear as the new formica-top desks replace the old wood ones. Therefore all the sex-related graffiti are being brought together in this article and what follows are uncensored samples of classroom graffiti, written but not signed, by various university students. The collection is a testament not only to college students' interest in sex but also to their ingenuity and their creativity.

What's the ultimate feminist sexual fantasy?
— *A vibrator that lectures on Marxism.*

To illustrate the innovative aspect of university graffiti, consider those sex-related graffiti where a word is broken in the wrong place, as in **It is better to have loved a short man, than never to have loved a tall** or **I like ass bestus**, where in the first case the *t* which belongs to the first word (*at all*) is placed on the second word instead (*a tall*), and in the second case the single word (*asbestos*) is divided in an unexpected way (*ass bestus*), which does not reflect the true make-up of the word.

Not only is there creativity at the word (or morphemic) level, but there is also great creativity at the sentence (or syntactic) level, as in **Use erogenous zone numbers**, where an expression is expanded by the addition of another word (*erogenous*), or as in **Have fun kids; it's later on you'll think**, where the expression "It's later than you think" is altered to give the new expression an entirely different effect. A graffiti dialogue goes:

> HE: *How do you like Kipling?*
> SHE: *I don't know, you naughty boy, I've never kippled!*

In this example the play on words is based on the *-ing* of Kipling's name. This has the same form as the *-ing* which marks a present participle, and therein lies the punning potential of Kipling's name. It is also possible to change the part of speech of a word without adding an ending at all. Everybody knows that in *meat loaf* the first word, *meat*, is a modifier of the noun *loaf*, but by changing the sentence, it is possible to make *meat* into a noun subject with *loaf* being the verb, as in **Don't let your meat loaf!**

Good graffiti writers are very careful in their word choices, with these choices more often than not being made on the basis of shock value. In such graffiti as **One man's queen is another man's sweathog** and **I did it in the privacy of my own crysalis while in metastasis**, the graffiti writer begins with set expressions and makes lexical substitutions into these expressions to change the tone, but in this case not the subject, of the expressions. This jarring relationship between particular words and the rest of the sentence can also be seen in **Let's be lewd** and in **Lassie is a bitch**.

One of the most common techniques of graffiti writers is the word play, or pun. Sometimes the word play is based on words which sound the same but are spelled differently, as in **Masseurs are people who knead people, Report obscene male — to obscene female** or **Go Hawaiian: Give your guy a lai**, where the play is based on the *need/knead*, *male/mail*, and *lay/lai* relationship. At other times the pun is based on a word which has two senses even though it has only a single spelling, as in **To go together is blessed; to come together is divine, It's all right to love a nun sometimes; just don't get into the habit, Coed dorms promote campus unrest** or **Raise the wages of sin**. One of the most common puns among graffiti writers is based on the multiple meanings of *screw* and related ideas as the following examples illustrate: **Alimony: The screwing you get for the screwing you got. — If Nixon would do to his wife what he's doing to the country, she'd be a lot happier. — Life is like a dick; when it's soft you can't beat it, and when it's hard you're getting fucked. — The earth is a whore and the human race is fornicating on her. — If you want a good screw, go to the local hardware store. — There are no virgins left; society has screwed us all.**

Sometimes the graffiti writer tries to force the reader into an indiscretion rather than writing the indiscretion himself. No one can read **Smuck fog** without being aware of the impending danger. There is even more potential for misreading something like **I am not the fig plucker but the fig plucker's son, and I can pluck figs until the fig plucker comes.** And the choice of the last word in **Nixon is a Cox sacker** was certainly as much on phonological as on semantic grounds. I am beginning to wonder if even such a harmless term as **Huck Finn** when written on a desk might have been written there in the hope that someone would mispronounce it.

University graffiti are not only full of lexical and phonological innovations, but logical innovations as well. Especially in the area of sex-related graffiti implication is common. What does the *it* refer to in **Motorcycles do it in the dirt**? Why would anyone want a person to **Vote for horizontal phone booths**? Just what kind of experience is being referred to in **I'm just an inexperienced little thing—looking for experience**? How would the graffiti reader know that the answer to the question **What goes in hard and comes out soft and sticky?** is "Bubblegum"? What high-frequency word has been omitted from **Yuck rhymes with: muck, duck, luck, buck, cluck, stuck, truck, tuck, etc.?** It is interesting that this same high-frequency word has also been omitted from *Webster's Third New International (Unabridged) Dictionary*. And exactly what is implied by the very slight alteration of the last word in **A jug of wine, a waterbed, and WOW!**? What is meant by the *something* of the following formula?

$$\begin{aligned} \male &= 0 \\ \male - \female &= 0 \\ \female - \male &= 0 \\ \female + \female &= 0 \\ \male + \male &= 0 \\ \female + \male &= something \end{aligned}$$

And finally, consider the implications of the following three-fourths of a poem:

I told him how to do it, how to hold his lips just so.
I told him to be ready when I gave the signal go.
He tried his best to please me, and he did as he was told.

The graffiti reader at this point is not sure exactly what is being implied, but he certainly assumes that it has something to do with sex, and is therefore surprised to read the last line:

But it's hard to learn to whistle, when you're
  only three years old.

What impressed us most about university sex-related graffiti was the number of subjects treated. They run the gamut from the perfectly acceptable topics of marriage, family life, dirty old men, and beauty through the controversial issues like birth control, overpopulation, and women's lib, and even extend into taboo areas like fetishes, sex-related diseases, homosexuality, incest, masturbation, prostitution, swinging, rape, and oral sex. These subjects will be treated in pretty much this same climactic order so that the reader can adjust gradually to the tone and wording, which in some cases may be shocking.

Marriage is a fairly frequent subject and puns are a frequent device, as in **Women without horse sense become nags** and **Statistics show great increases in marriages. Life seems to be just a marry chase.** Other statements are based on unusual logic that ranges from tautology, as in **Marriage is the prime cause of divorce**, to incongruity, as in **Stamp out first marriages.** In between there are all kinds of logical strangenesses like **A wife who can't cook and won't is better than one who can't cook and will**, **Don't marry for money: you can borrow it cheaper**, or **The marriage ceremony is a knot which is tied by your tongue, but which cannot be untied by your teeth.** Most of the marriage statements have a negative tone to them, as in **Let our priests marry; it will give them a working description of hell.**

To graffiti writers, the family is not an institution above criticism, as can be seen in **He who is henpecked may lend ear to other chicks, Richard Nixon can't stand pat**, or **Night Student, where is your wife now?** But in their usual technique of semantic inversion (putting good words in bad environments and bad words in good environments), writers reverse some of the old stereotypes, as in **I'm not a dirty old man, I'm just a sexy senior citizen** and **Bridge the generation gap. Turn an old man on.** The subject of beauty is also susceptible to semantic inversion, as in **Donna shaves her legs with a chain saw, You were never lovelier—and I think it's a shame!** and **Figures show that the average woman spends 75% of her time sitting down.**

We now come to the controversial issues like birth control. Some of the graffiti are in support of having children, as illustrated by **Support National Motherhood Week: Make one today!** or **May all your hang-ups be drip-dry** and **May all your consequences be little ones.** But most graffiti about having children are about not having them, as the following examples indicate: **Birth control is a high fly.** — **Make love, not children.** — **Orange juice for birth control; not before or after, but instead of.** — **Support planned parenthood now — before Mary has another lamb.** — **Tiny Tim wears a chastity belt.** — **Beware of Greeks bearing Trojans.** — **Nixon, pull out like your father should have.** — **The trouble with Nixon is that when he** withdraws, he only sticks it in again someplace else. — **True planned parenthood is kidnapping.** — **Pope Paul leads a rhythm band.** — **Accidents cause people.** — **Familiarity breeds contempt — and children.**

Much of the graffiti supporting birth control make special reference to "that pill," "the pill," or "a pill," which need not be further identified, as in: **Gather ye rosebuds while ye may, but take that little pill each day.** — **Pop the pill for pleasure.** — **Pope Paul pops the pill.** — **The pill: a gadget to be used in any conceivable circumstance.** — **A pill in time saves nine... months.** — **A pill a day keeps the stork away.**

When the unwanted pregnancy occurs, graffiti writers advise **Look homeward pregnant angel.** They ask **Would you be more careful if it were you who got pregnant?** And on the subject of overpopulation they write **Overpopulation begins in the home**, **Overpopulation is everybody's baby**, and **Children should be seen and not had.** But even though university students seem to be for birth control (or at least planned parenthood), and are against overpopulation, most of them seem also to be against abortion, as shown by **Abortion is hard on little babies.** — **Abortion: Legalized murder.** — **Abortion is murder.** — **Abortion: Pick on somebody your own size!** and **Aren't you glad you weren't aborted?**

College students are as confused as everyone else is about the feminist movement, as shown by the question **Are the women in this country really revolting?** The male chauvinist point of view is apparent in **Women's lib is okay—I just wouldn't want my sister to marry one**, **There's only two ways to handle women, and no one knows either one of them**, **Join Male Chauvinism!**, **Rise up sisters!**—*Rather difficult for a sister, isn't it?*, and **UNI women read books.** One example refers to the movement itself in **Women's Lib is a Msleading organization.** Compare this to the graffito representing the women's viewpoint **Women's Lib is NOW.** Other graffiti representing the female viewpoint include **Pray to God and SHE will help you**, **A Woman's work is never done—or recognized, or paid for, or honored, or commended...**, **Beware chauvinists! Today's pig is tomorrow's bacon** and **You'll never be the man your mother** was. Perhaps these last examples were not written by advocates of women's rights because they are rather flippant in tone, and it seems that most feminists are more serious. But at any rate, the male chauvinists and the women's libbers would probably both rally to the single graffito **Ban the bra!** but for entirely different reasons.

The bra is not the only article of clothing that appears in university graffiti. Some clothing goes up, as in **Up with skirts** and **Up the mini**. Other clothing goes down, as in **Down with pants!**, **Down with fig leaves**, **Down with zippers**, and **Hemlines are coming down; expect to hear some thighs of relief**, with this last graffito obviously having been written from the female point of view. And there are still other references to clothes, as in **Mickey Mouse loves the Minnie**, and **Sigmund's wife wore Freudian slips**. There are also graffiti that refer to no clothing at all, as in **Shame on the naked truth**, and **Those who sleep in the raw are in for a nude awakening**.

Various types of fetishes are also represented in graffiti. Clothing is mentioned in such graffiti as **George Washington wore ribbons in his wig**, and **Barry Goldwater wears pink underwear**. A shoe fetishist is defined as **A man who looks downward when he hears, "Gee, what a pair!"** There are also graffiti representing fetishes for various parts of the body. For knees there is **I'm in love with your knees!**; for thighs there is **Is the thigh the limit?** and **Able Mable Thunderthighs**; for the lips there is **Pat is a frog, cuz that is how he kisses**; for the derrière there is **Lady Godiva's ride made her cheeks rosy**, and **Anal erotics are behind us all the way**. It will probably surprise no one that the part of the anatomy most referred to, directly or indirectly, is the breasts. The following are representative: **Mother Earth is not flat**. — **Eva Gabor wears a training bra**. — **I don't care if your name *is* Napoleon, get your hand out of my blouse**. — **Raquel Welch wears falsies**. — **Aunt Jemima is stacked**. — **Raquel Welch is a stuffed shirt**. — **Hugh Hefner keeps abreast of the times**. — **Two men walking abreast**.

Hair is also an important topic for graffiti writers. Referring to the type that grows on the top of the head there is

Brunettes forever, Redheads are for everyone, and The average Blonde has an I.Q. equaling that of a medium-sized radish —from experiments conducted at the University of Michigan. The other type of hair is referred to in Puberty is a hair-raising experience, Richard Nixon is a pubic hair in the teeth of America, and Lower the age of puberty. And since we are in that region of the body, we will add two rather astute observations: It takes leather balls to play rugby and Santa Claus has pop-corn balls.

It is as if Santa had a disease of some sort—and indeed there are sex-related diseases that appear in the writings of graffitists: VD is God's perfect punishment for promiscuity, VD: The gift that keeps on giving, and VD is nothing to clap about. In the graffiti there is also reference to The girl from Emphysema, and it is rumored that Books give you syphilis. But there is a positive side as well, as when you are admonished to Hire the morally handicapped, or when you are told that Mononucleosis can be fun. It is heart-warming to know that Moby Dick and Grape Nuts are not social diseases. Probably the sex-related illness that affects the most university students is menstruation. Kotex is defined as Carpeting in the playroom, and Tampax as Manhole covers.

Men's sexuality received a small amount of desk space, as in Zap! You're sterile, and as when the three stages of man are listed in chronological order as Tri-weekly, Try weekly, and Try weakly! We were surprised to find no graffiti mentioning frigidity. Perhaps it has something to do with the age of the writers that they were more concerned with virginity, as the following illustrate: Chaste makes waste. — Virtue is its own punishment. — Have you heard about Joe and his girl friend? He called her Virge for short, but not for long. — Olive Oil is not a virgin — Sweet Pea is popeye's kid. — To the virgins: Thanks for nothing. — Virginity can be cured. Pledge yourself now. Give until it hurts. — Virginity is like a bubble on the ocean — one prick and it's gone forever. — Virginity is not incurable. — Fighting for peace is like screwing for chastity. — Mrs. Robert Kennedy is a virgin. — Impatient virgins never die. They just lose their cherry pie.

This last example is a play on the expression, "Old soldiers never die, they just fade away," but the graffiti writer has taken so many liberties with the expression that it is difficult to see the relationship to the original. Two graffiti that are superficially quite similar are **James Bond is a virgin** and **Grumpy is a virgin**. These two graffiti seem to be the same except that different names are used in the subject position. There is a further similarity in that these names are both masculine, even though there is an incompatibility between males and the concept of virginity. But logically, these two statements are very different. The people being referred to are not random males. James Bond was chosen because of all males he is probably the least likely to actually be a virgin. Grumpy was chosen because of all males he is probably the most likely to actually be a virgin, and furthermore, this explains why he is Grumpy.

One of the favorite sex topics of graffiti writers is homosexuality. Sometimes the expression *homosexual* or *homo* is written into the graffito, as in **My mother made me a homosexual, bless her heart**, or as in the dialogue *Enke is a homo.* **— He is not. —** *I am too*, or as in the misinterpreted syntactic and semantic graffito, **My mother made me a homosexual. —** *Would she make me one too if I brought her the yarn?* At other times the word *gay* is used, normally as a pun, as in **Ben Gay is hot for your body**, or **The Gay Nineties took place in Greenwich Village**, or **Go gay!** and **Nobody loves you when you're old and gay**. There is even a graffito poem that is based on the ambivalent meaning of *gay* as well as on many other words that have both sexual and nonsexual connotations:

I'm so happy, I'm so gay
That's cause I come twice a day.
I'm your mailman.
Knock your knockers,
Ring your bells.
Gee, I bet you think I'm swell.
I can come in any weather
Cause my bags are made of leather.
I don't need no keys or locks,
I just slip it in your box.
I'm your mailman.

There are other homosexual terms used like the *queer* in **I'm near enuf if you're queer enuf; I'll die laughing while you die trying**, and the *faggot* in **Support Birth Control! Become a faggot**. At other times there is no direct mention, only an implication, as in **My mom dresses me funny**, or **Denny Hoffman loves Tom Chapman; strange but true**. Then there are the homosexual graffiti where there is a certain logical incompatibility, as in **Tiny Tim wears a cross-your-heart bra**, and **My Aunt Harold has a problem**.

Let us now turn to some lesbian graffiti. There is **Have you thanked a lesbian today for not contributing to the world's population explosion?**, **George Wallace is a Jane**, and **All men at Harvard are homosexual except one, and he's a lesbian**. The expression from the lesbian vocabulary that is used most often is *dildo*. There is the **Dildo depth gauge**, the **Dildo floodlight attachment**, and for Christmas we are admonished to give a **Sheaffer pen and dildo set**. But the most mind-boggling reference to this item is the **Goodyear dildo blimp**, and the most homosexual of all is the simple and succinct autosexual statement **I love Me!!!** which brings us to the subject of masturbation.

Graffiti writers may pun in this area: **Do you think masturbation will get out of hand?** They may imply: **If it hangs, fondle it**. They may metaphorize: **An acid trip is mental masturbation followed by spiritual orgasm**. Or they may hypothesize: **I think I've fallen in love with my hand.** — *Thank God you're not ambidextrous*. The reader must supply his own interpretation to this last graffito. If a person were ambidextrous, would this introduce a third party in a love triangle or would it just provide a situation with too much sex (if that's possible) or what?

The most salient quality of incest graffiti is the recurring theme of family togetherness. These graffiti are typically very pleasant and positive in tone: **Incest: A game the whole family can play.** — **Incest and charity are alike; they both start at home.** — **Incest: A family affair.** — **Incest begins at home.** — **Incest is best.** — **Incest is best kept in the family.** — **Incest is like watching TV—the whole family does it**. We found only one exception to this light, airy treatment of incest: **Oedipus was a mother fucker!**

Most of the graffiti relating to prostitution are merely language play with the value system of the writer not reaching the surface. In **Casanova was a pimp**, and **Joe Namath is a pimp for Truman Capote**, there is merely a surprising incompatibility between the subject and the activity being referred to. In **A madam is one who offers vice to the lovelorn** there is a pun on *advice*. Most of the graffiti either take prostitution for granted, as in the above examples, or else are in favor of it, as in **Be ready to serve your country; be a call girl!** and **Support free enterprise; legalize prostitution**. The only statement that put prostitution in a negative light was **Pollution, like prostitution, is any departure from purity**.

There was an occasional reference to swinging, such as **John loves Mary; too bad he's married to Sue**, **Love thy neighbor, but don't get caught**, and **Jane sits home while Tarzan swings**, but judging from the small number of statements that we found on this subject, swinging is not very important to university students. Rape, on the other hand, is fully represented. In a graffito that has something of the same effect as the end of Shakespeare's *King Lear*, a dirty old man is defined as **a person who rapes a deaf-mute, and then cuts off her fingers so she won't tell**. Then there was the simple incongruity, **Rape — I'll vote for that**, the understatement **Rape is inconsiderate**, and the pun **Rape is an unnegotiated peace**. The definition of Russian Rape as **Ivan Toratitov** has syntactic ramifications since the name "Toratitov" can be viewed as either one word or four. Sometimes there is a comparison of rape with seduction, which after all, have certain aspects in common. For example, there's **Patience is the difference between rape and seduction**, and **Rape: Seduction without salesmanship**. One rape graffito which seems to make sense yet doesn't quite is **Fighting for peace is like raping for war!** Perhaps the writer copied it from **Fighting for peace is like raping for love**, but got confused.

Since graffiti are written anonymously, even a subject as taboo as oral sex can be treated. We are told to **Try to be a** sucksess, and **Milking machines suck**. We are even told that **There is no gravity; the world sucks**. And we are furthermore told that **Nixon had to see *Deep Throat* three times before he got it down pat**, and in pseudo-story-telling form we are told, **Meanwhile back at the oasis the Arabs were eating their dates**. We can see the effect of advertising on graffiti writers in **If he kissed you once will he kiss you again? Be sure! Use Vespray Feminine Hygiene Deodorant**.

Commercials have had an important effect on sex-graffiti in general. The *sex* in **A day without sex is like a day without sunshine**, and SEX: **Breakfast of champions** was not there in the original versions, nor was *Spanish Fly* in the original version of **Spanish Fly makes better loving through chemistry**. In some cases the product name remains a part of the graffito, as in **Love is like Jello; there's always room for more**, and **Colonel Sanders' wife is a cock raiser** and **Colonel Sanders says "The only way to get a better piece of chicken is to be a rooster."** What better endorsement could he have for his "fingerlicking" product? Then there are the graffiti which have commercial overtones in a more general way, as in **This chair is rated G(IRLS)**, **Sin now—pay later!** and **You may not approve of free love, but you've gotta admit the price is right**.

In comparing graffiti about love and sex, it appears that the love graffiti are typically more tender, as in **Lay down, I think I love you**. — **Love's just not in the making, but in the knowing**. — **Lovers, like bees, enjoy a life of honey**. — **Buy land, but invest in love**. — **Milk-drinkers make better lovers**. — **I never met a nympho I couldn't love**. — **Love 'em all; you might miss a good one**, or the succinct and somewhat poetic **Love is neato peato**, and finally the philosophical,

> *If you love something, set it free.*
> *If it returns, it's yours.*
> *If not, it never was.*

Sometimes the love graffito is a bit more flippant, as when we are told that **Sweden is a nice place to visit, but I would not want to love there**, **If loving is an art, we should all aspire to be Picasso**, and **Remember Girls, the way to a man's heart** is through the left ventricle. Or when we are let in on the following dialogue: **Love is of God.** — *God?* — **Yes, God.** — **Well, I'll be damned!** — **Probably.**

There are some negative love graffiti, as in **It's better to have loved and lost**—**much better, Love is a four-letter word,** and **Love isn't the answer; it's the problem.** But the preponderance of love graffiti is positive and the general philosophy of graffiti writers seems to be **Make love, not war,** or better put, **When the Power of Love overcomes the Love of Power, there will be peace.**

The graffiti related to sex in general have a similarly positive tone to them. Some of it is based on puns like **Of all my relations, I like sex best, Sex isn't good for one; but it's great for two,** or **Into the valley of death rode the sex hungry.** Some have a special phonological ring, as **Sex is emotion in motion.** Some relate to university life like **Preserve wildlife—throw a party, Conserve water; shower with your steady, Leda's lover is a quack,** or **My place or yours?** Some graffiti are negative (or fake negative) assertions like **Too much sex affects the vision,** or **Sex is like a snowfall**—**You're never sure how many inches you'll get.** Some are positive assertions, like **Candy is sweet, but sex doesn't rot your teeth,** and **Sex is good exercise.** Some are in the form of questions, like **Is there sex after death?** or **Remember when the air was clean and sex was dirty?** Indeed, just as there seems to be no end to the variety of sex, there seems to be no end to the variety of sex graffiti. And the exciting thing about it is that it's constantly being created all over so that by the time this is published, there will already be new examples just waiting to be collected.

ACKNOWLEDGMENT

My appreciation goes to Frank J. D'Angelo, one of the greatest graffiti collectors of all time, for his help on this article.

[*Editor's Note*: This article was submitted in March, 1977; thus the many dated anti-Nixon graffiti.]

Dialogue Graffiti

The following chain of graffiti, most of them written by different hands, was copied verbatim from the men's room (third floor) in the Life Sciences Building at the University of California, Berkeley, 2 August 1985:

The sultry bitch with the fiery eyes
The bulky bitch with thunderous thighs
The horny bitch who goes for guys
The topless bitch who digs French fries
The unwashed bitch who attracts flies
The romantic bitch with the lonesome sighs
The executive bitch w/ the striped ties
The ugly bitch who nevertheless tries
The not-cooking bitch who makes my bread rise
The sleezy bitch who the prudes despise
The robot bitch you computerize
The oriental bitch w/ slanted eyes
The rich bitch who always buys
The feminist bitch who will circumcise
The micro bitch who seduces flies
There's not a hitch to this misogynist kitsch
The transvestite bitch to the mensroom hies
The racist bitch for redneck guys
The post-doc bitch who ain't so wise
The starry-eyed bitch w/ warehouse eyes
The vampire bitch who never dies
The gorgon bitch who petrifies
The prostitute bitch who her trade plies
The warm-fronted bitch w/ the overcast skies
The falsy-topped bitch whose outline's a lie
The dead bitch who grossly putrifies
The AIDS tainted bitch was my slow demise
The Nympho-bitch w/ the orgasmic cries

(Contributed by Professor Rudolf Schmid, Botany Department, University of California, Berkeley.)

Disturbing Your Seed
or, Greater Love Hath Onan

Scott Beach

According to Eric Partridge's masterful *Origins*, "to masturbate" comes from the Vulgate Latin *masturbare*, whose past participle is *masturbatus*, whence "to masturbate." *Mas*- refers to the male seed (cf. *mas*culine, e*mas*culate), while *-turbate* has the same source as dis*turb* or per*turb*. Accordingly, when you jack off, assuming you're male, you're "disturbing your seed." If you're female, on the other hand, you should, by rights, have a word of your own. How about "cliturbate"? A neolojizm!

Now that we've laid the groundwork for this disquisition, let us consider the remarkable variety of terms, euphemisms, and phrases for autoerotism. Some are arcane and clinical, like **autoerotism**, some are pejorative, like **self-abuse**, and many more are simply ribald, like "**Yank my doodle, it's a dandy!**"

Probably the most popular of all expressions for this sublime activity is **jack off**, sometimes reduced to **j/o**. The "off" is clearly a reference to the climax of the ceremony. In other words, if you do it without having an orgasm, you merely jack. There are several other expressions with *off*: **jerk off, beat off, whack off, pound off,** and **do yourself off.**

A good many of these expressions incorporate terms of violence — *beat, whack, flog, pound, jerk, whip.* "An' there I was, **floggin' my log**, when...." "There wasn't anybody else around, so I decided **to whip it.**" "Wanna watch me **pound my pork?**"

Why are niggers always playing with their dicks?
—*Because that's the only thing the white man has left them.*

What do you call Arnold Schwarzenegger engaging in autoeroticism?
— *Onan, The Barbarian.*

Still others are more poetic: **make love with Mother Thumb and her four daughters**; **shake hands with the guy that stood up when I got married.** When a guy gets horny, and doesn't feel like having company, he can always **haul his own ashes.**

There is a controversial story in the Bible about Onan spilling his seed. In Genesis 38:9, we read: "And Onan knew that the seed should not be his; and it came to pass, when he went in, unto his brother's wife, that he spilled *it* on the ground, lest that he should give seed to his brother." In the very next verse, we read that this pissed off the Lord, wherefore He slew Onan. Verily, jacking off can be dangerous to thy health!

About 1590, somebody invented the coarse term **frig.** Apparently, it referred to friction, an indispensable ingredient in the act. Later, in the 18th century, someone else added *it*, as in "frig it!"

The French *se tapper la colonne*, meaning to tap, hit or pound one's column, has evolved into the usually insulting term *tapette*. If a Frenchman calls you a *tapette*, he means you're a jack-off.

Other English phrases are more rarified. **Prime your pump, stir your stew,** and **pound your pud** are cases in point. **Pull your wire** has an industrial connotation, and was possibly coined by an electrician experiencing a tumescence.

Many readers will recall the classic line: "Ninety-five percent of all males jack off, and the five percent who say they don't are damned liars." I, of course, have no way of proving that, one way or another. I suspect, however, that the author wasn't far off the mark.

What can we learn from all this? Well, what the hell do we *need* to learn? We're human... so we jack off! Big deal! It would be fair to say that if all the energy that goes into jacking off, world-wide, every hour of the day, could be harnessed, there'd be enough power to tell the Arabs and other oil producers to **go beat their meat!**

Why does Helen Keller masturbate with only one hand?
—*Because she needs the other one to moan.*

Offensive Language via Computer

Reinhold Aman

Computer networks can be used to gather information from throughout the world. Unlike in traditional fieldwork, one does not have to interview informants personally but simply posts a query, or an entire questionnaire, on the electronic *bulletin board* (BB), and the users respond.

To test the usefulness of his system, Mr. Birdseye asked his BB users about terms for masturbation. Following below are the terms, after organizing and alphabetizing the raw data.

to masturbate (of females): beat the beaver, buttonhole, clap your clit, cook cucumbers, grease the gash, hide the hotdog, hit the slit, hose your hole, juice your sluice, make waves [from "the (little) man in the boat" = clitoris?], pet the poodle, slam the clam, stump-jump.

to masturbate (of males): beat the bishop, beat your little brother, beat the meat, burp the worm, butter your corn, choke the chicken, clean your rifle, consult Dr. Jerkoff, crank your shank, dink your slinky, feel in your pocket for your big hairy rocket, file your fun-rod, fist your mister, flex your sex, flog the dolphin, flog your dog, grease your pipe, hack your mack, hump your hose, jerkin' the gherkin, please your pisser, point your social finger, polish your sword, pound the pud, pound your flounder, prompt your porpoise, prune the fifth limb, pull the pope, pull your taffy, run your hand up the flagpole, shine your pole, shoot the tadpoles, slakin' the bacon, slam your hammer, slam your Spam, slap your wapper, spank the monkey, spank the salami, strike the pink match, stroke the dog, stroke your poker, talk with Rosy Palm and her five little sisters, tickle your pickle, thump your pumper, tweak your twinkie, unclog the pipes, varnish your pole, walk the dog, watch the eyelid movies, wax your dolphin, whip your dripper, whizzin' jizzum, wonk your conker, yang your wang, yank the yam, yank your crank.

Postmature Orgastrix

Reinhold Aman

According to female and quasi-male academics, male-oriented language has been a major reason for the inequality of women, keeping them with this tool in an inferior position (not to be confused with the Missionary Position). For instance, we have *spinster* but no equivalent for "unmarried older man." We can now *do* something about this inequality by creating terminology of female equivalents hitherto ignored by the chauvinist oinkers. Unlike their opponents, those shifty-eyed males suffering from sexual identity problems who mouth support for women's equality — thereby hoping for a grateful lay from fierce & frustrated feminists — I don't just pay lip service, as it were, to genuine equality. For example, elsewhere in this volume I have coined *clit-cheese*, the female equivalent of the male's *prick-cheese*.

In this excursion to sexolinguistics, seven new terms will be introduced to provide exact, scientific labels for the eight possible situations encountered in sexual intercourse. Equal attention has been given to the male and the female. Now, at last, the most glaring *lacuna*, the female equivalent of the male "premature ejaculation," has been filled.

"Premature ejaculation" of the male occurs before the "proper" or "normal" time. This is, of course, a very subjective but commonly held notion. The man's timing may well

---

Why does the Jewish American Princess prefer intercourse dog-style?
— *Because she hates to see anyone else have a good time.*

be "proper" or "normal" but is "too early" only in relation to the length of the woman reaching her orgasm. If it takes the female sex-partner 30 minutes or more to reach an orgasm, most ejaculations would have to be labeled "premature." The man's alleged "premature" ejaculation is belittled and has a *terminus technicus*, whereas the woman's slowness in reaching an orgasm is accepted as "standard" or "normal" and thus lacks a pejorative label.

The term *praecox* is derived from Latin *prae* "before, early" and *coquere* "to cook," thus meaning "ripe/done before its time".

Note the seven holes, or gaps, in our language grid: we have no term for the female equivalent, nor any terms for orgasm occurring *at* the correct time, *after* the correct time, or *not at all*:

		M	F
pre-	*before* the correct time	+	−
—	at the correct time	−	−
post-	*after* the correct time	−	−
im-	at *no* time	−	−

Thus, to fill these gaps in our linguistic pattern, I should like to propose the following complementary terminology for all possible situations; note that here "ejaculation" refers to male orgasm, and "climax" to female orgasm:

MAN

premature ejaculation (*ejaculatio praecox*): ejaculation by the male *before* the woman reaches an orgasm (climax). Our standard, and only, term. Woman's most common reason for lamenting.

mature ejaculation (*ejaculatio cox*): ejaculation by the male *during* or shortly after the woman's climax. A normal woman's dream.

postmature ejaculation (*ejaculatio postcox*): ejaculation by the male long *after* the woman's climax. Relatively uncommon. A horny woman's dream.

immature ejaculation (*ejaculatio noncox*): non-occurrence of ejaculation by the male. Not to be confused with *impotence*.

WOMAN

premature orgasm (*climax praecox*): orgasm by the woman *before* the man ejaculates. Every man's dream. Very rare.

mature orgasm (*climax cox*): orgasm by the woman *at the same time* the male ejaculates. A staple fantasy of erotic and pornographic writings and movies. Extremely rare in real life and—like the long-dicked dorks of porno movies—the cause of much male anxiety and sexual dysfunction.

postmature orgasm (*climax postcox*): orgasm by the woman long *after* the male has ejaculated and turned flaccid. The most common situation, especially in married couples, and a major cause why males go a-philandering, hoping to find the rare Premature Orgastrix.

immature orgasm (*climax noncox*): non-occurrence of orgasm by the female. Not to be confused with *frigidity*.

With these seven new, scientifically correct terms, we have not only filled linguistic gaps but have also provided the much-needed medical terminology to classify real-life situations, hitherto neglected by all sexual researchers.

When a male is blamed for "premature" ejaculation, he can now counter the attack by accusing his female partner of "postmature" orgasm, thus projecting his uncalled-for guilt-feelings onto her. However, rather than trading sexual insults, such as "You postmature orgastrix!" or "You're just a postmature orgasmette!", one would lead a healthier sex-life if one delayed or sped up one's orgasm. Those prone to "postmature" orgasms can reach orgasm quickly by fantasizing about indecent acts with sheep or doorknobs, while their "premature" counterparts can delay their orgasms by thinking of such chilling sex-partners as Bella Abzug or Henry Kissinger.

The Sex Life of Micro & Millie

One night when his charge was exceptionally high, Micro Farad decided to seek out a cute little coil to let him discharge.

He picked up Millie Amp and took her for a ride on his megacycle. They rode across the Wheatstone bridge by the sine waves, and stopped in a magnetic field by a flowing current.

Micro Farad, attracted by Millie Amp's characteristic curves, soon was fully charged and had his field excited. He had her resistance to a minimum. He laid her on a ground potential, raised her frequency and lowered her capacitance.

He pulled out his high voltage probe, inserted it in her socket, connecting them in parallel, and began short-circuiting her resistance shunt. Fully excited, Millie mumbled, "MHO, MHO, give me MHO."

With his tube operating at a maximum peak, and her field vibrating with his current flow, Millie Amp soon reached her saturation point. The excessive current flow caused her shunt to overheat, and Micro Farad rapidly discharged and drained every electron.

They fluxed all night, trying various connections and sockets until his magnet had a soft core and lost all its field strength.

Afterwards, Millie Amp tried self-induction and damaged her solenoid. With his battery fully discharged, Micro Farad was unable to excite his generator. So they spent the rest of the night reversing polarity and blowing each other's fuse.

—*Author unknown*
[Southfield, Michigan, 1979]

License Plate Taboos

Frank Nuessel

Automobile license plates serve two primary purposes: motor vehicle identification and the generation of state and local revenues. During the 1970s, the latter function was supplemented by the enactment of legislation which permits the sale of so-called personalized or vanity plates at additional cost (ranging from $10.00 in Wisconsin to $100.00 in Hawaii and North Dakota). Most states normally permit a maximum of six characters (upper case Roman letters and Arabic numerals) on the six-by-twelve rectangular individualized tags. More recently, however, certain states (California, New Jersey and New York) have begun using up to eight symbols.

Vanity license plates are extremely interesting contemporary linguistic documents since they provide unusual evidence of various shortening devices.[1] Three specific abbreviatory mechanisms are widely employed. First is the deletion of orthographic symbols which may include the elision of vowels before the so-called liquid and nasal consonants (*l, r, n*), e.g. **REALTR**[2] 'Realtor' or in high-recognition brand names, e.g. **STDBKR** 'Studebaker.' Next is phonetic substitution which involves the use of the actual phonetic value of a letter or number as a part of a lexical item or a phrase which exceed the six or seven character limit, e.g. **EDUC8R** 'educator' and **10SN1** 'Tennis, anyone?'

What's the difference between a new bride and a new job?
— *After six months, the new job still sucks.*

Finally, initials and acronyms are used, e.g. **RJW** 'Robert Jay Wagner' and **OB GYN** 'obstetrician-gynecologist.'

In addition to the insights into shortening techniques, the official prohibition of certain combinations of letters and numbers on license plates, whether random sequential or potential requests for vanity tags, provides sociolinguistic evidence on censorship at the state level. The American Association of Motor Vehicle Administrators headquartered in Washington, D.C. has assembled lists of objectionable combinations of symbols which it has gathered from various state motor vehicle offices. In a recent article published in the Magazine section of *The Indianapolis Star*, Richard Pritchett discussed many humorous examples of the often arbitrary nature of such censorship.[3] Unfortunately, editorial constraints prevented Pritchett from including examples of many of the taboo combinations. Upon written request, the AAMVA sent me four separate lists (California, New York, Virginia and one unidentified state) of forbidden sequences. To a certain extent, these prohibitions offer insights into national and regional social taboos and preoccupations.

The proscribed semantic domains are fairly predictable. The following fields are included with representative samples. Each column corresponds to the total number of elements (three to seven).

I. Anatomy

ARS	BALL	BOOBS
ASS	COCK	GONAD
BUM	PRIC	PRICK
BUN	PRIK	PUBES
BUT	PRIX	PUSSI
CAN	TITT	PUSSY
COC		TITTS
DIK		TITTY

JUG
KOX
PUD
TIT

II. Drugs
LSD
RUM
POT

III. Excretory Functions
PEE   SHIT
PIS
SHT

IV. Exhortations

FUY	OHEL	EATME	4QUEUE	BULLSHT
HEL	USOB	LAYME	SHUVIT	BULSHIT
DAM	QQQQ	LEYME	SKRUIT	OMYGOD
			STIKIT	UPYOURS
			STUFIT	
			SUCKIT	

V. Ethnic/Racial Slurs

HUN	DAGO	COONASS
JAP	GOOK	NIGGAR
JEW		NIGGER
JIG		NIGGIR
MEX
NIG
WOP
YID

VI. Foreign Words

CON 'cunt'	**MERDE** 'shit'	**CABRON** 'cuckold'
CUL 'ass'		**CHINGA** 'fuck'
		COITUS 'sexual intercourse'
		LAPUTA 'the whore'
		MICULO 'my ass'
		MIERDA 'shit'

VII. Government Organizations

CIA	**USGOVT**
FBI	**USMAIL**
	KGBCIA

VIII. Questions

RUEZ2
RUGAY

IX. Religion

GOD	**JESUS**	**IAMGOD**

X. Sexual Preference

GAYBIRD
GAYGUY
GAYLIB
GAYSOK
GFAIRY
LESBIN
LSBEAN
LSBIAN

XI. Sex Acts (some of which may be exhortations)

FOC	SUCK	4NCATE
FOK	SUKK	
FUC	SUXS	
FUG		
FUK		
PET		
SUC		
SUK		
SUX		

NOTES

1. See Louis G. Heller and James Macris, "A Typology of Shortening Devices," *American Speech* 43 (1968), 201-208. See also John Algeo, "The Acronym and Its Cogeners," in *The First Lacus Forum 1974*, ed. Adam Makkai and Valerie Makkai (Columbia, S.C.: Hornbeam Press, 1975), 217-234.

2. All exemplary citations are attested forms and will appear in upper-case type.

3. Richard Pritchett, "Keeping Sex Off the Highway," *Star Magazine, The Indianapolis Star*, 18 October 1981, p. 22.

Have you heard about the Watermelon Patch Doll?
— *You buy one, send in the certificate, and you'll get welfare papers.*

What's the most dangerous job in Poland?
— *Riding shotgun on a garbage truck.*

Why do Polacks keep two dimes in their rubbers?
— *So that if they can't come, they'll call.*

Howard University Law School Final Exam

I. CONSTITUTIONAL LAW

A dude commit armed robbery. After he be arrested, the dude be hungry and ax the police to get him some chicken wings and a RC Cola. The police refuse and give him a bologna sandwich and water instead. Has the dude's constitutional rights been violated?

II. BANKRUPTCY

Lionel wish to open a bean pie factory. He borrow $100,000 from the SBA. One week later, Lionel file a bankruptcy petition due to economic fluctuations. Can Lionel keep his Cadillac?

III. DOMESTIC RELATIONS

Sylvester have not paid his non-support money to Yolanda for his and Yolanda's 14 children. This weekend, Sylvester want to take the children to the Coliseum to see the Jackson Five. Can Yolanda refuse to let Sylvester take the children?

IV. BANKING AND FINANCE

Clifton rob the Consolidated Bank and be running down Clay Street with the Man in hot pursuit. When Clifton hear the dogs and siren less than 50 feet away, he observe Tyrone walking out Slaughter's Lobby. He saunter up to Tyrone with sweat pouring down his face and looking over his shoulder and say "Say, Brother, would you like to purchase $50,000 worth of readily negotiable securities for $25.00?" Whereupon Ty, an economic adviser for HUD, say, "I'll give you $20.00 now and $5.00 next week." Clifton then consummate the transaction with the "right-on" handshake and black power salute.

(1) If Ty be caught, can he give Bondsman Elkins the securities to hold as collateral for his bond?

(2) Can Clifton consider the $5.00 that Ty owe him as accounts receivable for the current tax year?

V. INSURANCE

Willard pass on to his final reward in a razor fight after procuring a debit insurance policy for $2,000.00. After a two-week period of bereavement, Lawyer Mimms meet with the family and friends to discuss the estate.

(1) Do Haverty's Furniture Company have a shot at the insurance proceeds?

(2) Willard have not cashed his last welfare check. Can his devoted friend Corroledda sign his name to the check and keep the money?

VI. REAL PROPERTY

Alphonso "Nite-Batch" Jones have not paid the property taxes on the house he inherit from his Uncle Billy Jones for the past 12 years. Before the Sheriff can sell the property, the stove in the living room ignite and reduce Nite-Batch's house to ashes.

(1) Under these unfortunate circumstances, do Nite-Batch still have to pay the taxes?

(2) How much time do Model Cities have to replace the house?

(3) If Nite-Batch park his Grand Prix with gangster whitewalls where the house used to be and live in it, do he have to pay real property tax on the Grand Prix?

VII. PATENTS AND COPYRIGHTS

Isador obtain a grant from the Federal Afro Studies Administration to study the impact of the automobile on the black man. He invent a swivel stand for his auto TV and apply for and receive a U.S. patent. While on a lecture tour, Ford Motor Credit Company successfully repossess his Mark IV.

(1) Would the Neighborhood Legal Aid Society be successful in their suit in U.S. District Court against Ford Motor Credit Company for patent infringement?

(2) Assuming Isador prevail in his suit, can he be reimbursed for Greyhound passage back to Richmond?

VIII. TORTS

Deaconess Alvina Jackson, unmarried, give birth in the Fellowship Hall of Zion Church to a boy, Hiawatha, who depart this life shortly after being born. Since Deaconess Jackson have been deprived of extra welfare money, can she sue the midwife, Sister Olivetta Simpson, for medical malpractice?

IX. MATHEMATICS

(1) The judge give a dude 20 years for selling smack, with 10 suspended. How much time do the dude have to serve?

(2) Alreatha have 100 food stamps. She steal 15 more from Violina and send 10 to Florida. How many food stamps do Alreatha have?

(3) Braxton have been in an automobile accident. He get Lawyer Smith to settle the case for $9,000.00. Lawyer Smith's fee be one-third. How much have Lawyer Smith rip Braxton off for?

X. BIOLOGY

Circle the animal which is not seafood: (a) Catfish (b) Heel (c) Crabs

Sickle Cell Anemia is caused by licking food stamps.
( ) True ( ) False

XI. SOCIAL STUDIES

Who founded the free clinic at the Medical College of Virginia?

What were the dudes' names who led the Attica revolt?

Name at least three of the Soledad Brothers.

In the space provided below, give a detailed account of black history in the United States before 1951.

(Submitted by P. Bernstein)

Blacks and Indians

Two black whores—or *hos*, as they call themselves—got tired of the winters in Detroit and Chicago and moved to Arizona. There they ran into a couple of Native American women. "Hey, you be Indians?" asked one. — "Why, yes. I'm a Navajo and my friend, Gray Dove, is an Arapaho." — "Well, sheee-it! If dat don't beat all. I be a Détroit ho, and Maizie Lou here be a Chicago ho!"

Three black ladies decided to hit the big time as a singing group. They tried to come up with a name for their group. "Lennon Sister," suggested one. The other thought of "Andrews Sisters." But big momma said that they couldn't use these names, as there already were singing groups with these names. "I know. We'll call ourselves 'The Three Niggers,' 'cause that's what they're gonna call us anyway."

Black lady patient to physician: "What's the best type of sanitary napkin to use?" — "What's your flow?" — "Linoleum."

An Indian is having a drink at the bar. Suddenly he points to the floor and says to the bartender, "Big black bug!" — "Well," says the bartender, "squash it!" – "No, not squaw shit. Big black bug!"

The Jimmy Carter Statue

Dear Friend:

We have the distinct honor of being on a committee for erecting a statue of Jimmy Carter in the Hall of Fame in Washington, D.C. To be able do this, we will have to raise five million dollars.

This erection committee was in a quandary where to place the statue. It was not wise to place it beside the statue of George Washington, who never told a lie, nor beside that of Franklin D. Roosevelt, who never told the truth, since Jimmy Carter could never tell the difference.

We finally decided to place it beside the statue of Christopher Columbus, the greatest Democrat of them all. After all, he left not knowing where he was going, and upon arriving, did not know where he was; he returned not knowing where he had been, and he did it all on borrowed money.

Over 5,000 years ago, Moses said to the children of Israel, "Pick up your shovels, mount your asses and camels, and I will lead you to the Promised Land." Nearly 5,000 years later, Roosevelt said, "Lay down your shovels, sit on your asses, and light up a Camel; this *is* the Promised Land!"

Now, Carter is stealing your shovels, kicking your asses, raising the price of your Camels, and mortgaging the Promised Land. If you are one of the few fortunate people who have any money left after paying taxes, we will expect a generous donation as a contribution to this worthwhile project.

Respectfully yours,

Ronald Reagan

P. S. It is said that President Carter is considering changing the Democratic Party Emblem from a Jackass to a Condom, because it stands for inflation, protects a bunch of pricks, halts production, and gives a false sense of security while one is being screwed.

—*Author unknown*
[Modified by R. A.]

Tom, Dick, and Hairy
Notes on Genital Pet Names

Martha Cornog

I am sitting in a room with about thirty women. We are all attending a session on "vaginal consciousness raising" at a conference entitled "A View Through the Speculum."[1] The session leader, a beautiful, vibrant woman of a "certain age," asks us each to give the word(s) we use for our own genitals.

"Vagina." — "Pussy." — "Pussy. Vagina." — "Cunt." — "Mama's box." — "Henrietta."

Some people, like the last two women, use pet names to refer to their genitals. In *Lady Chatterley's Lover*,[2] the fictional Mellors calls his penis "John Thomas"[3] and Constance Chatterley's vulva "Lady Jane." Names like these (*Mama's Box, Henrietta, John Thomas*) I call genital pet names. They function as proper names[4] and refer to an *individual's* genitals only. In this way, they differ from general slang terms for genitals (e.g., *pussy, bearded clam, box; dick, cock, hog, one-eyed wonder worm*)[5] because they are personal, proper names.

Not only fictional characters like Mellors use pet names: real people name their genitals, too. To date, I have collected over thirty such pet names.[6]

The information given with each pet name follows this pattern (where supplied): significance or meaning of name; circumstances of naming or "christening"; the age of the owner of the genital at the time the name was used; and location.

When does a cub scout become a boy scout?
—*After he eats his first Brownie.*

Why do blacks wear high-heeled shoes?
—*So they don't scrape their knuckles when they walk.*

PET NAMES FOR THE PENIS

Alice: "Put Alice in Wonderland." From Lewis Carroll's book. *See* **Wonderland**. Private language between lovers.

Baby: "Does Baby want to go Home?" *See* **Home**. Private language between lovers. Age 20. Indiana.

Broom: Couple undergoing marriage counseling (*see* text, below). Indiana.

Casey: After Casey Jones, the brave engineer, who took a trip "into the promised land." Private language between lovers. Named by the woman. Age 20. Rhode Island.

Chuck: Middle name of owner. Private language between lovers. Named by the woman during sex play. Age 33. Ohio.

Dipstick: Couple undergoing marriage counseling. Indiana.

Driveshaft: Couple undergoing marriage counseling. Indiana.

Four on the Floor: A car's gearshift. Couple undergoing marriage counseling. Indiana.

Gearstick: Couple undergoing marriage counseling. Indiana.

George: "Let George do it." Age 24. Pennsylvania.

Gnarled Tree Trunk (G.T.T. for short): Shape of penis (heavily veined). Private language between lovers. Named by the woman during sex play. Age 50. Pennsylvania.

Hank: Named by owner at male drinking party (*see* text, below). Age 60. Pennsylvania.

Jason: London, England.[7]

Jawillbemy: Possibly a shortening of "Jane will be my. . ." Private language of flirtation (couple were not lovers). Age 18. Oklahoma.

Lazarus: "He rises from the dead." Age 33. Washington, D.C.

Little Weese: "Weese" is a Midwestern mispronunciation of owner's surname. Private language within intimate network of three couples. Age 20. Ohio.

Little Willy: Owner named Bill. "Little" is ironic, as "Little Willy" is nine inches long, according to Bill's ex-wife.

Mortimer: Private language between lovers. Named by the woman during sex play. Age 28. Ohio. *See* **Eunice**, below.

Periwinkle: Private language between lovers. May have been used previously by the man.

Peter J. Firestone: "Peter" from common slang for penis,[8] "J. Firestone" from middle initial and last name of owner. Private language between lovers. Age 18. Ohio.

Putz: Yiddish for "penis." Private language within intimate network of three couples. Age 20. Ohio.

Sniffles: Man had slight genital discharge; doctor suggested that maybe he had "caught a cold." Private language between lovers. Age 20. Toronto, Canada. Man (informant) is originally from the U.K.

Winston: "Tastes good, like a cigarette should." Private language between lovers. Age 30. Pennsylvania.

Zeke: Private language within intimate network of three couples. Age 20. Ohio.

▼ ▼ ▼

PET NAMES FOR THE VULVA[9]

Eunice: Old-fashioned name, corresponding to **Mortimer** (*see* above). Private language between lovers. Named by the man during sex play. Ohio.

Henrietta: Pennsylvania.

Home: "Does Baby want to go Home?" *See* **Baby**. Private language between lovers. Age 20. Indiana.

Honeypot: Couple undergoing marriage counseling. Indiana.

Little Monkey: "Can I pet the Little Monkey?" Couple undergoing marriage couseling. Indiana.

Mama's Box: Age 35. Pennsylvania.

Rochester: From the city where she lost her virginity. Private language within intimate network of three couples. Age 20. Ohio.

Virginia Vagina: Alliteration. Private language within intimate network of three couples. Age 20. Ohio.

Wonderland: "Put Alice in Wonderland." *See* **Alice**. Private language between lovers.

Although this list of names is not long, we can discern some patterns of naming, particularly for the penis. Most names of penises fall into one of the following categories:

1. A variation of the owner's name (*Little Willy, Chuck, Peter J. Firestone*).

2. A name suggesting a joke or catchy phrase, usually alluding to erection or sex acts (*Lazarus, Winston*).

3. What Sanders and Robinson call "power slang" [10] (*Driveshaft, Four on the Floor*).

4. Human first names that appealed or occurred to the namer for no reason that could be recalled by the informant. "The Saturday night of Opening Day [of trout season] I can remember vividly. [My father] he was drunker than a warthog.... We get out on the porch [to urinate] and he's...singing 'I took my organ to the party,'...he gets his fly open... and he starts to relieve himself—a fairly steady stream—and he starts talking to his organ and, by God, he calls the thing 'Hank.' He says, 'Aw, look at old Hank here, poor, poor old guy.' And he says, 'You and I, we've been in a couple of tight places together and we've had our ups and downs, but I want you to know, you old sonofabitch'—and this is where he starts shaking it off—'that I outlived you!'... That was the first time I had heard him allude to 'Hank' [and] I think it was just a spur-of-the-moment thing."

Some of the same patterns occur among the names for vulvas (*Wonderland*, for example). However, I have collected too few names for vulvas to be able to generalize at this point.

Who names genitals? In those cases where I was told the full story by the informant of the "christening" (16 cases out of 33), it was most often a group or couple interaction, or the other partner who produced the name. (For the remaining cases, this information was not available.) Penises seem to be named more often than vulvas.

Why do some people give proper names to genitals? After all, no one names feet, hands or elbows. Genital proper or pet names serve one or more functions.

First, the name(s) can serve as a private language between lovers or other groups of people who know each other well. Such a language permits discussion of sexual matters in front of unknowing friends and parents. The woman who told me about *Peter J. Firestone* said, "We would be sitting at dinner [with his parents] and he would toss off this comment, 'Well, maybe we could double-date with Peter tonight,' and then we'd go, 'Ha, ha, ha,' and hope that his mother didn't see me turn red!" Similarly, the owner of *Winston* and his girlfriend took great pleasure in discussing "Winston's good taste" in front of friends and relatives. One sex manual advises genital naming for this purpose:

> Pat your man's penis during nonsexual moments. Give it a pet name such as "John Thomas," used by Lawrence's Lady Chatterley; or name it after its owner, calling it "Junior" — "David, Junior," "Mark, Junior," etc. A girl I know has long hilarious conversations with someone named Penis Desmond — P.D., for short — who answers her in a high-pitched falsetto voice. This little act is a fun way to humanize a woman's relationship to a man's penis.[11] [Note that here the woman partner is advised to do the naming, and to pick a variation of the owner's name.]

When Sanders and Robinson solicited genital terms from college students, they found that the spouse/lover context elicited the greatest number of idiosyncratic responses, including pet names. To explain this, they quote Mark L. Knapp (*Social Intercourse*, Boston: Allyn and Bacon, 1978, p. 15): "The process of constructing a more intimate relationship eventually reaches the point where we are interacting with the other person as a unique individual rather than as a member of a particular society. Uniqueness in communication simply suggests the adoption of a more idiosyncratic communication system adapted to the peculiar nature of the interacting parties.[12]

In a broader sense, the pet name can also serve as a method of facilitating communication about sex. Many people, particularly women, are uncomfortable with the common generic terms for genitals.[13] One of my informants was a marriage counselor for several years:

> One of the things we frequently encountered were persons who were having a great deal of difficulty verbally communicating

about sex, and the reason was that they were extremely...uncomfortable with what they considered to be profane words, and they were uncomfortable with the official Latin terminology. And what was typically going on, then, was just nothing. With lack of a label, people weren't talking. So...after playing around with it for a while, I thought about the possibility of using made-up words. So we started doing that in therapy [having the couples make up names for body parts and sex acts] and we found it to be very successful. A lot of couples who had had trouble before really got into it, found it very enjoyable and developed a whole new vocabulary for sex organs and sexual acts.... From a therapeutic point of view, it was a very good idea, because, in addition to giving them a label that they could use to communicate and increase the effectiveness of what they were doing,...it [also] created a very nice thing for them to do together. The process of thinking up names and developing this new vocabulary was a very enjoyable process of sharing for most of the couples that tried it.[14]

Finally, the pet name bestows an identity upon the genitals: they have a personality which *is distinct* from the identity of the owner:

> The experience of genital excitation parallels the experience of the I in that it has a somewhat detached quality.... In men the penis is often given a name to indicate that it has a degree of independence from the self. It may be called "John," or *le petit homme* [the little man], or "Peter," to denote this independence from the self.[15]

Much current popular literature on sex and psychology describes the alienation and the love/hate relationship men often have with their penises: "...He curses his penis for not performing, as he sweats and strains and informs his partner that *he* really wants to, even though something is wrong with *it*."[16] And Jerry Rubin gives the dialog:

> *My penis:* I don't want to get turned on here. This bed is not safe for me.
> *My mind:* Shut up! Perform! Don't let me down!... You're humiliating me in front of Rosalie![17]

A man having some of these feelings who gives a pet name to his penis can thereby both wash his hands of what "it" does and also diffuse his anxiety through humor. Lawrence's Mellors illustrates this process:

> The man [Mellors] looked down in silence at the tense phallos, that did not change. — "Ay!" he said at last, in a little voice, "Ay ma lad! tha'art thee right enough. Yi, the mun rear thy head! Theer on thy own, eh? an' ta'es no count o' nob'dy! Tha ma'es nowt o' me, John Thomas. Art boss? of me? Eh well, tha'rt more cocky than me, an' that says less. John Thomas! Dost want *her*? Dost want my lady Jane?... Tell Lady Jane tha wants cunt, John Thomas...."[18]

Thus, we have the theme of genitals-as-personality. We can also call this "genitomorphism." It goes much further than the practice of giving proper names to genitals. It reaches into psychology, folklore, literature, art and religion. Included in this theme of genitomorphism are the subthemes of talking genitals (Thompson Motif D1610.6), genitals *talked to* and genitals acting on their own volition. Finally, of course, we have Genital Gods, i.e., phallic worship. Above, I have noted some of the psychological correlates of naming genitals. Gershon Legman discusses the folklore of genitomorphism. In his *Rationale of the Dirty Joke* (First and Second Series), he provides nearly twenty jokes or tales dealing with genitals named, speaking, spoken to, or acting on their own. Several examples, condensed here:

1. Groom on honeymoon to bride: "Honey, would you like to see *Oliver Twist*?"
   Bride: "Why not? I've seen it do everything else!"
2. Prostitute sees reflection of her vulva in a puddle: "There you is, you l'il ol' money-maker!"
3. Man amputates penis accidentally while shaving. Severed penis: "I know we've had lots of fist fights in our time, but I never thought you'd pull a knife on me!"[19]

And a wonderful cartoon was described to me, reportedly published in *The Realist*, of a man holding his penis, *which is saying* (via a cartoon "balloon"), "Not tonight, dear, I have a headache!"[20]

In literature, I have already mentioned *Lady Chatterley's*

Lover. I have found other interesting examples. In *Portnoy's Complaint*, Portnoy has a long dialog with "the maniac who speaks into the microphone of my jockey shorts."[21] Henry Miller, in *Tropic of Capricorn*, gives a long and detailed typology of "cunt personalities."[22] The hero of Petronius's *Satyricon*, Encolpius, has a violent argument with "a part of me which no serious man thinks worthy of his thoughts."[23] Legman cites several additional references from literature.[24]

In the graphic arts, genitals have been depicted as self-contained beings, or as the heads of otherwise human bodies. Fourteen plates in *The Complete Book of Erotic Art* depict this theme,[25] including a delightful series of Japanese prints of a Sumo wrestling match between a penis and a vulva, which ends (not surprisingly) with the penis being engulfed by the vulva/vagina.

Finally, a substantial literature concerns phallic worship. Edwardes gives one example in *The Jewel in the Lotus*, where he describes "the evil *jinee El-A'awer* (one-eyed penis genie), patron spirit of the ravisher."[26]

As Vance Randolph and Gershon Legman point out, "a fascinating monograph could be written on these themes of the speaking privates of both sexes...."[27] Genitals *named*, genitals *spoken to*, genitals *acting independently*, and genitals *deified* are related themes. All are subsumed under the broader concept of "genitals-as-personality." But we have yet to understand fully why genitals are personified, the cultural conditions under which personification happens and, finally, what it means to people who say *Henrietta* or *Winston* to genitals.

FOOTNOTES

1. A View Through the Speculum: A Workshop on Vaginal Health and Politics. Sponsored by the Elizabeth Blackwell Health Center for Women. Philadelphia, Pa., May 17, 1980.

2. David Herbert Lawrence. *Lady Chatterley's Lover* (New York: New American Library, 1959), pp. 196-97, 212-14, 283.

3. "John Thomas" is also generalized slang for the penis, as quoted from *The Pearl* by Tim Healey in "A New Erotic

Vocabulary," *Maledicta* 4(2):191, Winter 1980. Mellors, however, uses it as a personal pet name.

4. "Proper names" are explained by David Schwarz as "semantic atoms. They cannot be constructed by a speaker out of pre-existing material; they must be learned individually." (*Naming and Referring: The Semantics and Pragmatics of Singular Terms* [New York: De Gruyter, 1979], p. 51.)

5. For additional terms for genitals, *see* Tim Healey's wonderful compendium [*op. cit.*, pp. 181-201] and "Naming the Vulvar Part" by Clyde Hankey [*Maledicta* 4 (2): 220-22, Winter 1980].

6. All owners and informants, with the exception of *Jason*'s and *Sniffles*'s owners, were U.S. citizens. None was self-identified as homosexual. I do not know if the patterns of genital naming by homosexuals are different in any way from heterosexual patterns.

7. *Jason* was the name a male stripper gave his penis, reported in "A Big Gland for the Little Ladies." [*Oui* 4(3) : 13, March 1975.] Was *Jason* looking for the Golden Fleece?

8. *Firestone* is a pseudonym for the surname of the owner.

9. I was going to call this section "Pet Names for the Vagina" until I read Mildred Ash's "The Vulva: A Psycholinguistic Problem" [*Maledicta* 4(2) : 213-19, Winter, 1980, with accompanying mnemonic].

10. Janet Sanders and William Robinson. "Talking and Not Talking About Sex." *Journal of Communication* 29(2):22-30, Spring, 1979, p. 28.

11. Xaviera Hollander. *Xaviera's Supersex: Her Personal Techniques for Total Lovemaking* (New York: New American Library, 1976), p. 134.

12. Sanders and Robinson. *Op. cit.*, p. 29.

13. Sanders and Robinson's data suggest that women have fewer terms for sexual parts and acts than men, and verbalize less about sex, particularly about their own genitals. (*Op. cit.*, pp. 27-28.)

14. David Weis. Personal communication. Dec. 12, 1980.

15. Alexander Lowen. *Fear of Life* (New York: Macmillan, 1980), p. 87.

16. Herb Goldberg. *The New Male: From Self-Destruction to Self-Care* (New York: William Morrow, 1979), p. 120.

17. Jerry Rubin and Mimi Leonard. *The War Between the Sheets* (New York: Richard Marek Publishers, 1980), p. 68.

18. Lawrence. *Op. cit.*, pp. 196-97.

19. Gershon Legman. *Rationale of the Dirty Joke: An Analysis of Sexual Humor.* First Series (New York: Grove Press, 1968), pp. 285-86, 301, 371, 490, 750-51. Second Series *No Laughing Matter* (New York: Breaking Point, 1975), pp. 169, 229, 236-37, 589, 597, 604-05, 629, 874-76, 878-89. One of these tales is treated at greater length in Vance Randolph and Gershon Legman, "The Magic Walking Stick," *Maledicta* 3(2): 175-76, Winter, 1979. The three jokes given come from First Series, p. 490 and Second Series, pp. 229, 605.

20. Arno Karlen. Personal communication. April 10, 1981.

21. Philip Roth. *Portnoy's Complaint* (New York: Random House, 1969), pp. 126-28. (Cited by Legman, *op. cit.*, Second Series, pp. 586-87.)

22. Henry Miller. *Tropic of Capricorn* (New York: Grove Press, 1961), pp. 194-95. (Cited by Legman, *op. cit.*, First Series, p. 371.)

23. Quoted by Robert S. De Ropp in *Sex Energy* (New York: Delacorte Press, 1969), p. 125.

24. Legman. *Op. cit.*, First Series, pp. 750-51; Second Series, p. 237.

25. Phyllis and Eberhard Kronhausen. *The Complete Book of Erotic Art*, Volumes 1 and 2 (New York: Bell Publishing, 1978); plates 146, 326 in Vol. 1; plates 23, 123, 130, 335, 337-46 in Vol. 2.

26. Allen Edwardes. *The Jewel in the Lotus* (New York: Julian Press, 1959), p. 109.

27. Randolph and Legman. *Op. cit.*, p. 175.

In what section of the newspaper do they print Polish obituaries?
— *Under "Civic Improvements."*

What does a Jewish American Princess do with her asshole every morning?
— *She sends him off to work.*

Ritual and Personal Insults in Stigmatized Subcultures

Stephen O. Murray

Although which attributes are considered pejorative may vary from culture to culture, speech acts recognized as insults probably exist in all cultures. Speech *events* involving sequences of insults are characteristically (though not exclusively) used by those whose silence is not cutting. For instance (1) is a speech event involving two children,

(1) A: **You're fat.**
    B: **Well, you're stupid, so there!**

comprised of two speech acts, both of which are insults. A labels B with a disvalued characteristic and B retaliates.

Ritual insults can be distinguished from such literal *personal* insults by the greater outlandishness of characterization, and by the chaining of successive insults. The negative characterization in a ritual insult is patently not true. This literal implausibility must be obvious to the participants. Particularly to the insulted person the "not serious" frame (Bateson 1972) must be made clear. Metaphorical exaggeration and rhyme are two means to signal the "playing insult" frame (Labov 1973:123). The second distinction between ritual and personal insults is that each retort is linked to the preceding insult, prototypically by rhyme, but also by building on the semantic foundation of the first insult or making a "play" on its words.

What's the biggest problem for a black nun adjusting to convent life?
— *Learning to use "Superior" after "Mother."*

The goal of the retorter[1] is to silence his[2] opponent — to "strike him dead" with "lightning" repartee. What constitutes an appropriate response to a personal insult differs from what constitutes an appropriate response to a ritual insult. The appropriate response to a personal insult is fight or flight if the insult is made by someone of relatively equivalent status, to passively "take" it from someone of superior status, or to ignore it (at least at the times of the interaction) from someone of inferior status (and to have the upstart punished later by someone else). A personal insult (to an adult) is overt aggression. In subcultures with exaggerated sense of personal honor, such as the white planter caste of the antebellum American South, or 19th-century European officer corps, an insult was a prelude to a duel.[3] A ritual insult, however, is an invitation to "play" in a contest of wits.[4] The appropriate response is verbal rather than physical violence. *Within* a group, violence in any form other than verbal is regarded as a failure to match wits. Playing with strangers risks misinterpretation of the frame and may lead to fights (Labov 1972; Kochman 1970). To deny a patently exaggerated statement with rational argumentation is just as silly (and hence damaging) as resorting to physical force.

According to Radcliffe-Brown (1940), in a joking relationship "one is by custom permitted and in some instances required to take no offense" (195), but "taking abuse," i.e., accepting the insult with aplomb, is not positively valued in ritual insult exchanges. There, aplomb is at most only of instrumental value: one must not become so upset as to be unable to think of a good retort. Good performance requires taking the offensive, and taking offense is an obstacle to that. In addition to this distinction between ritual insults and joking relationships in terms of response, the two differ in participants. Joking relationships exist between persons in some set structural relationship (e.g., if one must accept denigrating jokes from mother's brother), whereas ritual insults are exchanges by peers. The locus of joking relationships is the family, whereas ritual insults occur in peer group idle hours (Abrahams 1962:219; Howell 1973).

Ritual insults occur in several North American subcultures. The one in which they are most prominent is that of urban black adolescents (Dollard 1939, Golightly and Scheffler 1948; Abrahams 1962; Kochman 1970; Mitchell-Kernan 1971; Labov 1972). A folk art form consisting of rhymed retorts has been found in black ghettoes across North America. Black youths who do badly in schools and are classified as "verbally deficient" show a highly developed linguistic competence along with verbal artistry and keen sociological and psychological perception in speech events of their vernacular culture, including ritual insults (Labov 1972, 1973). In the simplest and most ubiquitous example,

(2) A: **Motherfucker!**
   B: *Your* **mother.**

B turns A's jibes back on A's family. Verbal deftness in twisting the original insult is highly prized. Escalating coarseness is common, but neither necessary nor sufficient. To somewhat simplify the rules for reply, given (a), (b) is a failure and (c) a success:

(3) A: $T(B)$ is x
   B: $T(A)$ is x
   C: $T(A)$ is y, and y is worse than x (Cf. Labov 1972)

in which T is the targeted person, A and B are speakers, x and y are insulting attributes. The insulted person (B) cannot simply repeat the same form, saying the insulter is also x, but must produce some other insulting characterization of A: y might be an escalation of x, a twist on it, or some other attribution from within the same semantic domain. Memory is more important than invention in "the heat of battle," at least for rhymed retorts; *ad hoc* responses likely sacrifice rhyme (reported already waning by Dollard 1939). However, ritual insults that are not rhymed are more difficult to recognize—for participants as for analysts. Unrhymed insults with the same content as rhymed insults are more likely to be taken seriously. So, although in one sense it is easier to play when the retorts do not need to rhyme, other distancing devices are needed to distinguish the game of ritual insults from the serious and sometimes lethal business of personal insults. More bizarre and outrageous forms of accusations are often relied upon to signal this distance.

TOPICS OF BLACK YOUTHS' RITUAL INSULTS

Reanalyzing the contents of the corpora of ritual insults reported in studies of the speech of black youths, one can see that the most frequently mentioned theme is sexual receptivity. That of one's mother is most frequent (as in 4), but the wantonness—or at least accessibility—of other relatives (5) or oneself (6) also occasion comment.

(4) **Your mother's like a police station: dicks going in and out all the time.** (Labov 1972:140)

(5) **It takes twelve barrels of water to make a steamboat run. It takes an elephant's dick to make your grandmammy come.** (Kochman 1970:158)

(6) **Roses are red. Violets are blue. I fucked your mama, and now it's for you.** (Abrahams 1962:212)

Blackness is a second theme of black ritual insults. Early work emphasized self-hatred and rejection of blackness both in the sense of skin color and in the sense of "country" or "low-down nigger" behavior. Insults such as "You so black you sweat Super Permalube oil" seem to denigrate blackness, but Kochman (1970:158) argued that whiteness—again, either shade or culture—may also be a target.

Abrahams (1962) similarly suggested that "aping" or "selling out to" white culture are weighty charges. Deviance from culturally appropriate behavior is not monotonic and varies from group to group. Labov (1972:133) reported the following whiteness insult:

(7) **Your mother so white she have to use Mighty White.**

A third major theme is poverty. Recurrent forms include **Yo' so poor..., Yo' family so poor..., Yo' mother eat..., Yo' mother raised you on...,** and **I went to your house and...** [some grotesque event occurred], e.g.,

(8) **I went to Money house and I walked in Money house. I say — I wanted to sit down, and then, you know, a roach jumped up and said, "Sorry, this seat is taken."** (Labov 1972:136-7)

(9) **Yo' moma eat Dog Yummies.**

Remarks like the last may be taken personally and lead to fights, denial, or flight — even within a peer group. Eating dogfood (9) is not outlandish in urban American ghettoes. Neither is the presence of cockroaches (8), so simply calling attention to such phenomena is not innovative. Greater than normal abundance or boldness must be asserted, as in (8).

Labov (1972:134-5) proposed the following as the basic black ritual insult form:

Your mother so ... she ....

Surprisingly, Labov's collection of ritual insults had a much narrower topic range than earlier, more impressionistic collections. In the insults Labov reported, only characteristics of mothers were mentioned (fathers in some retorts). Another common topic, according to Abrahams (1962:211) is homosexuality of fathers or brothers, e.g.,

Your brother like a grocery store: he take meat in the back.

Dollard (1939:5) also noted incest and passive homosexuality as "frequent themes." In passing, Labov (1972:166) mentioned a "large class of ritual insults which impute homosexuality to the antagonist," but he apparently ignored those data. Thus, mothers are not the only topic of black youths' insults, although they may be mentioned in all three of the classes here suggested: sexual receptivity, blackness, and poverty.

DEVELOPMENTAL INTERPRETATIONS

Adolescents, especially urban black male adolescents, must learn to defend themselves in the hostile world outside the home. Dollard (1939), Abrahams (1962), and Kochman (1970) regarded ritual insults as conditioning the victim to rough treatment. While taunting may train one to maintain composure (Goffman 1957), this is only a negative precondition for success in insult interchanges. The retort is the positive accomplishment. Insult interchanges provide training for the fast-thinking, fast-talking skills used to outwit and out-talk representatives of the dominant social order, such as welfare workers, police, schoolteachers, and hostile majority group members encountered in unofficial interaction.

Cutting loose from the mother (the dominating socializing force in early years) is a part of growing up emphasized in accounts of black insults. Ridiculing femininity and weakness may be means to independence, to masculinity (Abrahams 1962:213-4; cf. Devereux 1937; Levy 1973), and to making the transition from mother-centered childhood to masculine peer-group-centered adolescence (Labov 1972). Mothers' expressed approval of masculinity and the general denigration of women in American culture facilitate this.

As Dollard (1939) recognized, projection also plays a large part: projection of homosexual feelings and of aggressive feelings about one's mother. She cannot be attacked, but peers' mothers can (Abrahams 1962:214).

Finally, the importance of play in the acquisition of communicative competence has been emphasized by Hymes's followers (see Bauman 1974, 1976; Kirshenblatt-Gimblett 1976).

To generalize statements about ritual insults as characteristic of stigmatized groups, the remainder of this essay reports exchanges of insults from the two other subcultures analyzed in *The Survival of Domination* (Adam 1978). The miniscule Jewish data were witnessed in Detroit. The more abundant gay data are drawn from naturally-occurring interactions in Toronto, Edmonton, Tucson, Detroit, and San Francisco.

TOPICS OF GAY RITUAL INSULTS

The three basic themes found in the content analysis of reported black ritual insults recur in gay insults, if a more general gloss is substituted for "blackness." Sexual receptivity, degree of conformity to the stigmatized culture, and relative income are more general categories capturing corpora from the two subcultures.

Unlike black ghetto boys, gay men do not usually make remarks about the mothers of those they wish to insult. As adults, usually not living with parents, their parents are not visible to prospective insulters. And having made the adolescent adjustment to leaving the childhood world of the mother, gay men are less obsessed with these problems—folk prejudice to the contrary notwithstanding.[5] Even among hustlers the same age as the black youths studied, mothers are not a topic.

The most common theme of black ritual insults is sexual receptivity. The sexual behavior of one's whole family can be of central concern to an adolescent, and is particularly likely to be in a culture where kinship is central and one is held responsible for the sexual behavior of other family members (see Carrier 1975; Glazer 1976), but for most American adults, only statements about the individual threaten one's reputation.

Contempt for sexual receptivity from the dominant culture is shared by some within the gay community,[6] as, indeed, are negative judgments about homosexuality itself (Ashley 1979, 1980). Stigmatized subcultures are by no means immune to the values and prejudices of the majority culture (Humphreys and Miller 1980; Mitchell-Kernan 1971; Ashley 1979:218).

Hayes (1977) and Ashley (1979, 1980) suggest that "camp" is dead, overestimating the homogeneity of the contemporary gay world. As Murray (1982) showed modeling disparate conceptualizations of "gay community,"[7] the advent of a "Stonewall generation" (i.e., those whose gay identity crystallized after the 1969 Greenwich Village riots) did not result in an overnight change of self-conception everywhere. Not only are there still "pre-Stonewall" queens, even in New York and San Francisco, but new ones are being socialized (what Robert Patrick termed "the queen machine"). Members of the "post-Stonewall" or "clone" generation are too committed to hyper-masculinity with its strong, silent presentation of self to engage in repartee on any topic. Indeed, conversation of any sort is markedly deviant in many encounters in the institutions of contemporary gay ghettoes. It must be kept in mind, therefore, that in what follows, a minority of a minority are being described. "Clones" may "camp" in some social gatherings, while "queens" are neither an extinct nor a vanishing species.

The classic queens accepted feminine labels, seizing thereby the advantage of being able to denigrate others' masculinity without defending their own. Being penetrable is one thing, but being too-penetrable is and was an attribute that can be targeted, as in the following:

(10) A: **We can't afford to lose another sofa** [disappearing up your distended anus].
B: **Your ass is so stretched you should put in a drawstring.**
A: **Word is you've had your dirt-shute mack-tacked.**
B: **And you wall-papered your womb.**
A: **Where do you find tricks who'll rim your colostomy?**
B: **You douche with Janitor in a Drum.**
A: **Slam your clam.**
B: **Slam it, cram it, ram it, oooh, but don't jam it.** [demonstrating]
A: **Cross your legs, your hemorrhoids are showing.**
B: **You need to strap yours forward so you'll have a basket.** [male genitalia implied otherwise lacking]
A: **Better than back-combing my pubies, like you do. Preparation H is a great lubricant.**
B: [pointing at *A*] **This girl's hung like an animal—a tsetse fly.**
A: **Four bulldogs couldn't chew off this monster.** [fondling himself]
B: **I don't think even a bulldog would want** *that* **in its mouth. Besides, I've seen chubbier clits.**
A: **Peeking under the door in the washroom again?**[8]

Most of the insults derogate the other's masculinity, although the "oooh" acknowledged that *B* was not adverse to getting fucked. From enlarged anuses the exchange moved to diminutive penises. In the following exchange *A* had just been fucked while *B*, his roommate, had been in the next room. *A* begins by implying that *B* had gone into the bathroom to masturbate:

(11) A: **Sitting on the toilet with your toy up you again?**
B: **Darling, you already have the only** *man* **in the house in you. He can't very well be two places at the same time—**
A: **And you** *do* **need to fill yourself with something.**
B: **What's it to you?** [a stop signal]
A: **But if you can't get anything that's alive, can't you at least get something that was alive once?**

B: Like what? Rob the morgue like you usually do?
A: Nah, they'd turn away. You wouldn't feel a carrot, what about a pumpkin?
B: What about *your* handle? [a come-on]
A: Not available.
B: Oh, no! [mock horror] You mean that hunk you're with is a woman like us?
A: Wouldn't you like to know?
B: How could I not know? I hear every thrust he makes and every gasp from you.
A: So you know, why ask?
B: Yeah, I know; your hands are in love with your cock.
A: Takes two hands to handle a Whopper.
B: That's why you'd be perfect for me.
A: Shit! They should shoot rockets up your ass. Then maybe you could feel it.
B: You mean if you fucked me I wouldn't feel anything?
A: You could try a shotgun. Bullet'd probably get lost, though.
B: You should get lost—or stick to taking it up the ass. You should put in a toll gate. Then we could pay the phone bill.[9]

In this exchange (not all of the speech acts being insults), *B* acknowledges not only sexual receptivity, but desire for *A*. The latter makes him vulnerable to rejection and *A* doesn't charge *B* with being receptive, but with being too fucked out to feel being fucked. Nor does *B* attack *A* for being fuckable (the masculine self-image of *C*, the guest, is, however, potentially open to comment).

Too much sexual activity of any sort may be a source of envy, and hence of comment, e.g.,

(12) A: It's time to pull in your horns. [inhuman phallic apparatus]
B: At least I can get it up. [in implied contrast to *A*'s impotence]

Not being able to attract men may be noted (as in 11), but attracting too many can also draw derogatory comment, as in the last thrust in (11) and

(13) A: Ships passing in the night have nothing on you.
B: Me? Your bedroom looks like the Hong Kong harbor—
A: Sailors smell sea food. [said in a bragging tone]
B: You forget: Hong Kong harbor is full of junks.

Looking worn-out is often attributed to sexual hyperactivity as in

(14) Where were you last night? Your eyes look like roadmaps.

Just as it is possible to be too black or not black enough, it is possible to be too overtly gay on the one hand, or to pretend not to be gay on the other. While there is clearly an overtness/covertness continuum, the appropriate place on it to be varies considerably in the opinion of cliques and individuals. In any milieu in which various gay networks are mixed (especially queens and clones), comment can be aroused by what is deemed inappropriate ("trashy") behavior. There is *no* level of overtness which cannot be faulted be someone as either "flaunting it" or as "trying to hide it." Still, it is the latter that occasions the "bitchiest" comment. "Closet queens" are said to wear "crystal veils," i.e., disguises transparent to other gay men. Closetry is an acceptable topic for insult among queens, clones, and even the most politically-correct politicos. The following examples all were produced by self-identified clones (in social gatherings):

(15) You're 'bout as straight as a fever chart in a malaria ward.
(16) You're about as straight as a rattlesnake ready to strike.
(17) You straight? Yeah, like Highway One curving up the California coast.

And then there is the retort to ostensibly straight researchers:

(18) Writing a book, eh? What better way to get material than on your knees. [i.e., in position to fellate]

In (19) the possibility of bisexuality is challenged:

(19) A: Nobody can dance at two weddings? Which is it?
B: How would you know? You can't dance at all?

The extended examples above include recurrent charges of being too overtly homosexual (a "flaming queen").

Pretensions other than to masculinity form the next most frequent class of insults, although they may revert to comments on pretensions to masculinity, as when one person in a gay bar was rhapsodizing about his new car, and the person beside him stage-whispered,

(20) Too bad he had to hock his cock. [get fucked rather than fuck to get it]

"Tackiness" rather than poverty is the charge applied to substandard expenditure as in

(21) Nice car, but where do you put it when they lock the park? [i.e., the target does not own a house with a garage; he spends his life engaged in sex in the bushes of public parks]
(22) Don't most parties include booze?

If value and taste must be granted, "piss elegance" can be invoked:

(23) Christ! You can't turn around in here without breaking something. [fragile antiques]

The rule seems to be, "If you can't deny it, devalue it." This rule applies to more than purchased objects. For instance, one well-hung man on the gay beach seemed overly proud of the size of his penis, so another commented (in another stage-whisper):

(24) That's no cock; it's just the handle to turn him over with. [cf. (11) on "handle"]

Also on the beach, the following exchange culminates in a devaluation:

(25) A: **I have him wrapped around my little finger.**
B: **The only thing you ever had wrapped around your finger was a piece of elastic to remind you who you are, and you lost that.**
A: **I get more men than you can count.** [possibly this could be interpreted as an insult to *B*'s mental ability, but it was probably intended as a personal insult]
B: **Tricks are for kids.**

In (26) another desirable condition (having a lover) is devalued:

(26) A: **You're like a railroad track: laid all over the country.** [apt because *B* had not been around of late]
B: **I got married.**
A: **Some old troll.**
B: **You ain't ever seen him.**
A: **Anyone who'd go with you I'd never look at; I know what he must look like to wanna fuck you. Who wants something looks like he already groun' up in the meat grinder?**
B: **Honey, I the meat grinder. You stick it up, I does the turning.**
A: **I'd be too 'fraid.**
B: **So lil' you'd get lost?**
A: **Ain't nobody ever called it little before.** [though swaggering, this breaks frame as argumentation rather than retort]
B: **Don't matter how big it is if you don't know how to use it.**[10]

B devalues penis size and *A* devalues having a lover.

Pretentiousness is a more global category than relative affluence, but charges of pretentiousness overlap charges about sexual identity and sexual behavior. Sexual identity, cultural identity, and relative affluence gloss non-overlapping categories; pretentiousness cross-cuts them just as attributes of mothers cross-cut black ritual insults.

CONTENT OF JEWISH RITUAL INSULTS

There are parallels to black and gay uses of ritual insults in North American Jewish communities, in which wit and quick repartee are also valued, and the same themes reappear. Sexually nonconforming behavior seems to be universal (although the norms for appropriate behavior vary). Second, just as it is possible to be too black or not black enough in appearance and behavior, or too overtly gay or too "closeted," it is possible to be judged too assimilated—"denying your heritage"—or too stereotypically Jewish. Lacking money or throwing it around are also occasions for insults. While informants make these generalizations, I have not collected examples, except the following about "denying one's heritage" and (horrors!) emulating blacks:

(27) A: Where dja get those shvartse clothes?
 B: At least I don't look like I just got off the boat!
 A: No? You look like you're getting *on* the boat—to Africa!
 B: Not everyone wants to look like a rabbi, you know.
 A: Something's wrong with rabbis? You're not Jewish anymore?...

This exchange took place in northwest Detroit (1977) between old friends who hadn't seen each other recently. Whereas *B* considered the opening sally as ritualized, *A* may not have been playing even with his first question. Clothes are, or course, an important symbol of cultural identity, and the entire conversation (including the discussion following the exchange quoted) dealt with what is the appropriate amount of Jewish visibility. Intra-familial discussions of this topic are a widely-noted feature of Jewish life in North America.

CONDITIONS FOR PLAYING

Black: The entire black population cannot be characterized by participation in ritual insulting. Labov (1972:255-

92) split the population of black urban youths into two groups: those who participate in gang street culture and those who do not. For the latter he borrowed the folk label "lame." "Lames" do not know the slang, nor how to verbally duel, and so on. This gross dichotomy is important, because it is a rare indication that many black youths do not command the vernacular, nor engage in the verbal games of that culture. Unfortunately, neither Labov nor other observers have estimated what proportion of the population is "lame."

Just as knights made careers of jousting, Southern gentlemen, *samurai*, and Prussian officers careers of dueling (Flynn 1977), some regular participants in subcultural settings build up a reputation for verbal dueling and become specialists within a network. In Labov's study, "Boot" stands out as the master craftsman of insults. His superiority at playing the game is recognized by other gang members, who often refuse to engage him in verbal duels. Since "communicative competence" is stratified, the recognized masters frequently must hold back, waiting for worthy opponents on whom to test their wits (teachers are reported to be too pathetic to bother with "showing them up").

Gay: Just as being a young urban black does not automatically imply participation in street culture or even passive knowledge of vernacular games, being gay does not automatically give one comprehension of gay argot or competence in verbal game-playing. Most self-styled "queens" have probably played insults, but not all are very good at being witty rather than gross. And most gay men would be insulted to be labeled "queens" and have never been involved in extended exchanges like those reported here. One part of the stereotype of gay people held by others is that they spend much of their time "bitching," "backbiting," "cutting each other down" (Adam 1978). Very few gay men and seemingly still fewer lesbians spend an appreciable amount of time verbally dueling. The rarity of ritual insults in the many hours of participant observation in gay political groups, in other "post-Stonewall" institutions and various gay circles suggests that only a minority of those who frequent gay settings engage in the sort of stylized repartee discussed here.[11]

There are a few specialists, like "Boot." On special occasions, one group's champion dirt-talker may do battle with another's specialist for entertainment of all, as in (10). Since not everyone is an active participant (and still fewer accomplished in the art), the question becomes, "Who will insult whom when and where?"

The first condition is that the insulter cannot be trying to pass as anything he is not—a social success, rich, or, especially, straight. Those passing do not want attention focused on them: they are too vulnerable to devastating rejoinders to wield weapons of insult in public (private expressions of contempt are another matter altogether).

Second, insulting seems to be a skill more developed among what might be called "the doubly damned"—black gays and gay transvestites. Both are likely to encounter denigrating remarks from other gay men as well as from straight people. A sharp tongue is a weapon honed through frequent exercise, and is a survival skill particularly of "drag queens." Generally, aggressive self-denigration is an art of oppressed people. It is not the black youths who lead sheltered lives ("lames") who "play the dozens," but, rather, those most exposed to racist aggression.

Third, insults seem more the provenance of older, more closeted gay men than of younger, publicly self-accepting gay men (although as noted above, there are young queens and young closet queens and the "arts of oppression" are not about to be lost). The variables of age and openness are confounded: young, closeted males may lack a peer group of likewise closeted friends, while older closeted men frequently have networks of closeted friends (Warren 1974; Covelli 1978), and some openly gay men have predominantly straight networks.

Generational differences can be attributed to a number of factors: greater self-acceptance, stronger group norms of self-acceptance, lower status ("less to lose"), less experience of "pre-Stonewall" self-loathing and repression, and the formative influence of gay liberation. The last dampened insults interpretable as self-loathing, but recourse to insults focused on "tackiness," "piss elegance" and closetry continued. The "post-Stonewall" or "clone" generation is distinctly less verbal, but people whose experience and outlook are "pre-Stonewall" continue to pour out of the provinces, the suburbs, and sometimes even cities with gay ghettos, so generation cannot easily be linked to age or birth order. Date of birth is less important to "generation" than when one came out: gay people of divergent ages who came out into a particular gay world belong to one generation, while two gay people of the same age who came out at different ages (may) belong to different generations. Access to information about the existence of other gay people, the presence of gay role models, and the particular experience of oppression and challenge to it affect *how* one is gay (not *whether* one is homosexual).

Standard sociological independent variables other than "generation" and "passing" do not seem to affect the distribution of insulters: not class, not education, though possibly race.

Having made these assertions about who plays, let us turn briefly to the questions of "when" and "to whom." The latter defied specification, because almost anyone can become the target for outlandish insults—friends, enemies, strangers. Anyone perceived as an affront to one's sensibility, a poacher on one's territory, or a potential rival may be targeted. Nevertheless, some individuals seem to be the butt of an inordinate share of insults.

Most gay ritual insults occur within exclusively gay settings. The presence of rivals of long standing or of regular targets accounts for many exchanges. New persons may become targets by breaching the expected order of the situation—especially if they are unaware of what that expected order is. "Tourists" or persons wandering into gay settings by accident are especially likely to be the victim of displays of wit and/or outrageous behavior (Cavan 1963; Lee 1978), displays for which they are rarely prepared with adequate retorts. If the insulter is mistaken in identifying a "tourist," more spirited retorts will be made.

Of the gay insults outside gay settings, many occur near gay territories. Against bypassers, "tourists," and "fag-bashers," tongues sharpened on peers cut loose on "straights." As Mezzrow and Wolfe (1969:198) noted of black adolescents

> What they were sharpening in all this verbal horseplay was their wits, the only weapon they had. Their sophistication didn't come out of moldy books and dicty colleges. It came from opening their eyes wide and gunning the world hard. [*Dicty* = black dialect for "pretentious vocabulary." –*Ed.*]

Various "queens"—especially those identifiable targets for straight aggression or with black skins—have been performing their own guerilla theater in the streets for a long time, using keen perception and sharp words to demand acceptance, or to annihilate any who would deny it. Such "play" is, quite literally, "self-defense." Although many denigrations stem from, and perpetuate, collective self-hatred, at least some undermine the oppressive cognitive structure, attacking those who deny the group. However much they may be practiced on stigmatized fellows, the skills of quick, acute perception of others and lighting repartee are used against the group's oppressors.

NOTES

A preliminary report of some of these data was presented at the 1977 annual meeting of the American Sociological Association in Chicago. The author wishes to acknowledge the encouragement and the comments of Niyi Akinnaso, Keith Basso, Philip Blumstein, Meredith Gould, Joseph Hayes, John Lee, Dennis Magill, Brian Miller, Terry Moss, Kenneth Payne, William Simon, and one of the anonymous referees for the *American Sociological Review*. The ignorance about ethnography and about the world revealed by other referees should be documented, but as is argued in this essay, it's no fun insulting the verbally incompetent. Nevertheless the idiocy of the demand for a "control group" from one referee for *Qualitative Sociology* must be mentioned.

1. Dittmar (1976:227) is simply wrong by claiming that "the whole point is to outdo the other in the coarseness of the insult."

2. The masculine pronoun is used throughout because both the existing literature and the observations reported here deal with male peer groups. Carolyn Dirksen, Meredith Gould and Deborah Spehn have assured me that black girls do not lack in ritualized repartee but have not provided examples.

3. "What was ritualized in dueling days was the glove-slap, whereupon the offended party gave to the offender the right to choose weapons. What the writer misses is that even when things went that far, an actual duel was not common—most got bogged down in preparations" (anonymous referee comment).

4. Joking was conceived by Radcliffe-Brown (1940) as a means to avoid conflict, but humorous sallies are examples of aggression and conflict, not conflict avoidance (Lyman 1971; Howell 1973).

5. As Adam (1978) showed, the dominant group projects a mother obsession on groups it inferiorizes: the omnivorous Jewish mother, the black matriarch, and the castrating homosexual-genic mother are all creations of the dominant group's imagination (see also Murray 1984).

6. Participants in stigmatized subcultures do not possess a wholly distinct culture (Mitchell-Kernan 1971; Humphreys and Miller 1980): one of the reasons for the prefix.

7. Consideration of "gay community" as a technical term is provided by Murray (1979).

8. This exchange followed a Canadian Thanksgiving dinner and involved two masters of the art both in their early 30s. They were performing for the other guests.

9. Both participants were in their late teens. The exchange was reconstructed, so this is not a direct transcription. However, *A* accepted it as capturing what had been said accurately (*B* shortly after the exchange evicted *A*).

10. Both participants were gay black males in their late teens. The exchange took place in the heart of the "valley of the clones," i.e., at Castro and 18th Streets in San Francisco.

11. In Guatemala City, Murray (1980) showed that the same terms for "homosexual" are not shared by those involved in homosexual cruising. Most of the terms in Rodgers (1972) and Ashley (1979, 1980) were unknown to San Francisco gay men I queried, although known generative principles allowed some to be decoded correctly.

REFERENCES

Abrahams, Roger D.
    1962   "Playing the Dozens," *Journal of American Folklore* 75:209-20.
    1974   "Black Talking in the Street," pp. 240-62 in R. Bauman and J. Sherzer, *Explorations in the Ethnography of Speaking*. Cambridge: University Press.

Adam, Barry D.
   1978   *The Survival of Domination.* New York: Elsevier.

Ashley, Leonard R. N.
   1979   "*Kinks and Queens*: Linguistic and Cultural Aspects of the Terminology for *Gays,*" *Maledicta* 3:215-55.
   1980   "'Lovely, Blooming, Fresh and Gay': The Onomastics of Camp," *Maledicta* 4:223-48.

Bateson, Gregory
   1972   *Steps to an Ecology of Mind.* San Francisco: Chandler.

Bauman, Richard
   1974   "Verbal Art as Performance," *American Anthropologist* 77:290-311.
   1976   "The Development of Competence in the Use of Solicitational Routines," *Working Papers in Sociolinguistics* 34:1-16.

Carrier, Joseph M.
   1975   "Urban Mexican Male Homosexual Encounters." Thesis, University of California, Irvine.

Cavan, Sherri
   1963   "Interaction in Home Territories," *Berkeley Journal of Sociology* 7:17-32.

Covelli, Lucille H.
   1976   "A Gay Friendship Network." Thesis, University of Toronto.

Devereux, George
   1937   "Institutionalized Homosexuality among the Mohave," *Human Biology* 7:498-527.

Dittmar, Norbert
   1976   *Sociolinguistics.* London: Arnold.

Dollard, John
   1939   "'The Dozens': Dialectic of Insults," *American Imago* 1:3-25.

Flynn, Charles P.
   1976   *Insult and Society.* Port Washington, NY: Kennikat.

Glazer, Mark
   1976   "On Verbal Dueling among Turkish Boys," *Journal of American Folklore* 89:88-91.

Goffman, Erving
   1957   "Embarrassment and Social Organization," *American Journal of Sociology* 62:264-71.
   1963   *Stigma.* Toronto: Prentice-Hall.

Golightly, Cornelius and Israel Scheffler
    1948   "Playing the Dozens," *Journal of Abnormal and Social Psychology* 34:104-5.
Howell, Richard W.
    1973   *Teasing Relationships.* Addison-Wesley Module 46.
Hayes, Joseph J.
    1977   "Language and Language Behavior of Lesbian Women and Gay Men." Ms.
Humphreys, Laud and Brian Miller
    1980   "Stigma and the Emergence of Culture," in J. Marmor, *Homosexual Behavior.* New York: Basic Books.
Kirshenblatt-Gimblett, Barbara
    1976   *Speech Play.* Philadelphia: University of Pennsylvania Press.
Kochman, Thomas
    1970   "Toward an Ethnography of Black-American Speech Behavior," pp. 145-62, in R. Whitten and J. Szwed, *Afro-American Anthropology.* New York: Free Press.
Labov, William
    1972   *Language in the Inner City.* Philadelphia: University of Pennsylvania Press.
    1973   "Linguistic Research in American Society," pp. 97-129, in E. Hamp, *Themes in Linguistics.* The Hague: Mouton.
Lee, John Alan
    1978   *Getting Sex.* Toronto: General.
Levy, Robert I.
    1973.   *The Tahitians.* Chicago: University Press.
Lyman, G. Peter
    1971   "On Male Chauvinist Humor," *Phalanstery Review* 3,10:9-11
Memmi, Alberto
    1968   *Dominated Man.* Boston: Beacon.
Mitchell-Kernan, Claudia
    1971   *Language Behavior in a Black Urban Community.* Berkeley: Language Behavior Research Laboratory.
Murray, Stephen O.
    1979   "Institutional Elaboration of a Quasi-Ethnic Community," *International Review of Modern Sociology* 9:165-77.
    1980   "Lexical and Institutional Elaboration: The 'Species Homosexual' in Guatemala," *Anthropological Linguistics* 22:177-85.
    1982   "Labels and Labeling: Prototype Semantics of 'Gay Community'." *Working Papers of the Language Behavior Research Laboratory* 51.

1984 "Psychoanalytic Fantasies in Black and Gay," in S. Murray (ed.), *Cultural Diversity and Homosexualities*. New York: Irvington.

Radcliffe-Brown, A.
1940 "On Joking Relationships," *Africa* 13:185-210.

Rodgers, Bruce
1972 *The Queens' Vernacular*. San Francisco: Straight Arrow.

Stanley, Julia P.
1970 "Homosexual Slang," *American Speech* 45:45-50.
1974 "Gay Slang, Gay Culture," American Anthropological Association meeting, Mexico, D.F.

Warren, Carol A. B.
1974 *Identity and Community in the Gay World*. New York: Wiley.

Linguistic Ambiguities

Two fellows are walking down the street when they see a dog licking his dick. The one says, "Damn! I wish *I* could do that!" His friend replies, "You probably can. But you better first pat him on the head."

A young priest strays into the red-light district. A prostitute comes up to him and offers him a blowjob for $40. Not knowing what a blowjob is, he keeps walking. Another hussy stops him and says, "Would you like a blowjob? Just forty bucks." The priest shakes his head and walks on. After a third whore offers him a blowjob for $40, he decides to go back to the convent. When he sees Mother Superior, he asks her bewildered: "Mother Superior, what's a 'blowjob'?" She says, "Forty bucks. Just like in town."

A Compilation of Jokes Offensive to Everyone

Why are there no black mountain climbers?
— *Because their lips explode at 5,000 feet.*

How do you say "Fuck you" in Jewish?
— *"Trust me."*

What's the perfect woman like?
— *She's three feet tall, doesn't have any teeth, and the top of her head is flat so you can put your beer down on it.*

What is a Polack no-hitter?
— *A wedding where the fights don't start until after the priest has left.*

What's the longest six years in a Negro's life?
— *Third grade.*

What do you call a faggot with a broken tooth?
— *An organ grinder.*

What's the difference between Nancy Reagan and a tampon?
— *No difference. They're both stuck up cunts.*

What evidence do we have that Adam and Eve were not black?
— *No one, including God, has ever been able to take a rib away from a nigger.*

Why are a woman's asshole and pussy so close together?
— *So when she gets drunk you can carry her home like a six-pack.*

What's a hillbilly virgin?
— *An eight-year-old who can run faster than her brothers.*

Why did so many black soldiers die in Vietnam?
— *Because when someone yelled "Get down!" they got up and danced.*

Why is San Francisco like granola?
— *Because once you get past the fruits and nuts, all you have left is flakes.*

What do you get when you cross a gorilla and a computer?
— *A Harry Reasoner.*

What goes into thirteen twice?
— *Roman Polanski.*

What's brown and full of holes?
— *Swiss shit.*

Why don't Polish women use vibrators?
— *Because they chip their teeth.*

What is a blood vessel?
— *Four Negroes in a '57 Chevy.*

Why were Helen Keller's legs yellow?
— *Because her dog was blind, too.*

Why do Italians wear pointed shoes?
— *So they can get the cockroaches in the corners.*

What's the cheapest way to grease your car?
— *Run over a Puerto Rican.*

Why did God make come white and urine yellow?
— *So that Italians could tell if they were coming or going.*

Did you hear about the flasher who wanted to retire?
— *He changed his mind and decided to stick it out another year.*

What's a concubone?
— *A male concubine.*

Who was the first soft-drink manufacturer?
— *Adam. In the Garden of Eden, he made Eve's cherry pop.*

Who was the first carpenter?
— *Eve. She made Adam's banana stand.*

What did the one gay sperm say to another gay sperm?
— *"How do you find an egg in all this shit?"*

What's the difference between a dyke and a lesbian?
— *The dyke kick-starts her dildo.*

What's the definition of a *rugged* woman?
— *One who kick-starts her own vibrator and rolls her own tampons.*

What does a gay whale do when he meets up with a submarine?
— *He bites off its tail and sucks out the seamen.*

Why did God create gentiles?
— *Well, somebody* has *to pay retail!*

Why did Jesus cross the road?
— *Because He was nailed to a chicken.*

What do you call a nun with one leg?
— *Hopalong Chastity.*

Why did the Baptists outlaw fucking?
— *Because it may lead to dancing.*

What did the Valley Girl say to the black before giving him a blowjob?
— *"Ooooh, gag me with a coon!"*

How do you pick out the Polish dykes at a lesbian convention?
— *They are the ones picking up men.*

What's the difference between Jewish women and the Bermuda Triangle?
— *The Bermuda Triangle swallows seamen.*

Why do blacks think about sex all the time?
— *You would, too, if you had a head full of pubic hair.*

Why do they call the camels the Ships of the Desert?
— *Because they are full of Arab seamen.*

Why do car salesmen call blacks "Doo-duhs"?
— *Because many black car buyers ask, "Do duh cah come wif a radio? Do duh cah come wif air conditionin'?"*

How do you bathe Haitians?
— *You don't. You just let them wash up on shore.*

What do you call a black hitchhiker?
— *Stranded.*

Why did the Wave want to get out of the Navy?
— *Because she found out that a 21-inch Admiral was a TV set.*

How do you babysit a black kid?
— *Wet his lips and stick him on the wall.*

Where did Prince Charles spend his wedding night?
— *In Diana.*

Why didn't the little Greek boy run away from home?
— *Because he couldn't leave his brothers behind.*

What's a Jewish porno film?
— *Ten minutes of sex and 50 minutes of guilt.*

Why do Jewish women use golden diaphragms?
— *Because they want their men to come into money.*

Name a biceptual athlete.
— *Arnold Schwarzenegger.*

Did you hear about the new German microwave oven?
— *It seats twelve.*

What's the difference between a Jew and a pizza?
— *A pizza doesn't scream when you stick it in the oven.*

How can you spot an Italian airplane?
— *Look for hair under its wings.*

How can you tell that a woman is wearing pantyhose?
— *When she farts, her ankles swell up.*

What do you call a gay Jew?
— *A Heblew.*

What do you call a black skindiver?
— *Jacques Custodian.*

What do you call a beautiful girl in Poland?
— *Tourist.*

What's black and white and has three eyes?
— *Sammy Davis, Jr. and his wife.*

What kind of meat do priests eat?
— *None.*

What's yellow and ugly and sleeps alone?
— *Yoko Ono.*

Why did God give blacks rhythm?
— *Because He fucked up their hair.*

How do you keep five blacks from raping a white girl?
— *Throw them a basketball.*

What do you get when you cross a Mexican with a faggot?
— *A señor-eater.*

How did Helen Keller's parents punish her?
— *They rearranged the furniture.*

What is Jewish foreplay?
— *Two hours of begging.*

How does a French girl hold her liquor?
— *By the ears.*

How do you fuck Elizabeth Taylor?
— *Roll her in flour and look for the wet spot.*

What's black and shines in the dark?
— *Oakland, California.*

Have you heard of the Jerry Falwell designer jeans?
— *They have one right leg and a welded zipper.*

What do you get when you cross an orangutan with Jerry Falwell?
— *An ignorant, uneducated asshole that likes bananas.*

Why didn't Jesus like to eat M&M's?
— *Because they kept falling through his hands.*

Why did the West Germans elect a new chancellor?
— *Because they were tired of the same old Schmidt.*

What's the difference between a vulture and a Jewish mother?
— *The vulture waits until you're dead before it eats your heart out.*

How can you tell when a Jewish American Princess has an orgasm?
— *She drops her nail file.*

What's black and white and has a dirty name?
— *Sister Mary Elizabeth Fuck.*

Did you hear about the gay rabbi?
— *He kept blowing his shofar.*

What's long, black, and has an asshole at each end?
— *The line at the welfare office.*

What does a French-Chinese prostitute do?
— *She sucks your laundry.*

What do you call an overweight Chinese?
— *Chunk.*

Why don't Frenchmen eat flies?
— *Because they can't get their little legs apart.*

What do Jackie Onassis and Bambi's mother have in common?
— *They both fuck for bucks.*

Why can't Santa Claus have any children?
— *Because he comes only once a year, and that's down the chimney.*

Why don't Polish cheerleaders do the splits?
— *Because they stick to the floor.*

How do you get four gays on a bar stool?
— *Turn it upside down.*

Have you heard about the queer burglar?
— *He couldn't blow the safe, so he went down on the elevator.*

Why can't you circumcise Iranians?
— *Because there is no end to those pricks.*

Why is Ray Charles smiling all the time?
— *Because he doesn't know he's black.*

How do you get 17 Yankees into a car?
— *Tell them it's heading for Houston.*

What do you get when you cross an Indian with a black?
— *A Sioux named "Boy."*

What do you get when you cross Bo Derek with Sammy Davis, Jr.?
— *A ten of spades.*

Viet-Speak

Dan Cragg

In February 1971, *The Army Reporter*, a military newspaper published under the auspices of the U.S. Army in Long Binh, South Vietnam, published a version of the Little Red Riding Hood fable couched in the language of "Viet-Speak." *Viet-Speak* is an ingenious neologism coined by an anonymous journalist on the *Reporter* staff that describes perfectly the linguistic salmagundi spoken by U.S. Armed Forces personnel who served in South Vietnam.

During the eleven years that significant numbers of U.S. troops participated in the Vietnam War, an eclectic vocabulary evolved as their own distinct lingo. It consisted of words passed on from much older times and wars that found new life in Vietnam; loan words from the Vietnamese language, often mispronounced and misunderstood by Americans; words borrowed by the Vietnamese from us and garbled in the most interesting ways; French, Chinese and Japanese borrowings; military jargon; peculiar nonce words and expressions; and wholesale appropriations from the lexicon of general American slang that through usage became the exclusive property of Vietnam veterans.

Viet-Speak was delivered in the "laid-back" cadence of young men inured by danger and hardship, men who knew how precious it is to have a safe place to shit, a dry pair of boots, and a tight pussy. It was a language that reflected

---

Why does Alabama have so many niggers and Buffalo so many Polacks?
—*Alabama had first choice.*

a devil-may-care intimacy with horror, spoken by men whose only objective was survival for the year they were in Vietnam and then — escape. Viet-Speak was the perfect complement to the affectations of war: graffiti-covered equipment; chests festooned with bandoleers of machine gun ammunition; outrageous moustaches; short haircuts; cheap cigars; good luck charms; peace symbols; firearms; sex; booze; drugs.

The philosophy of the Vietnam soldier, if he could be said to have had one at all, was quite simple. His friends and neighbors had sent him to what he considered the *anus mundi*, so how could anything worse happen to him? "What're they gonna do, ship me to Vietnam?" was his invariable reply to any suggestion that he might get in trouble over something. Thus Viet-Speak reflected the sardonic pessimism of soldiers who knew instinctively that they had been sent to fight a war shackled with restrictions imposed by pettifoggers who would not have to share the blame if things went wrong.

The Little Red Riding Hood story is a very neat metaphor for the whole Vietnam "experience." In it we come face to face with deep-rooted fears concerning ravishment, duplicity, tragedy and death. But Hood survives, even if her rescue is somewhat *deus ex machina*, and the Vietnam soldier knew that he too would survive. The nation also survived Vietnam and although it's no longer spoken, Viet-Speak lives now in our Vietnam War literature, waiting. The youngest Vietnam vets are still in their 20s and they'll be telling their stories well into the middle of the next century.

For obvious reasons, the unknown reporter who wrote the first Viet-Speak story had to be circumspect in his choice of words and the vocabulary he used to write about them. Fortunately, this being a scholarly paper, I have exercised complete academic freedom and rewritten the original story the way it really would have been spoken. Viet-Speak deserves to be chronicled.

To that anonymous Army journalist on the staff of *The Reporter*, well, my *Gabby Hayes* has long since crumbled into dust, but permit me to tip it figuratively and wish him, wherever he may be, indoor plumbing, dry feet — and *cold cees* three times a day!

As our story begins, Little Red Riding Hood is leaving her hooch[1] in the vil[2] with a doggie pack[3] of chop,[4] consisting mostly of cold cees,[5] to take to her sick grandma-san.[6] As she skips merrily through the punji[7] traps to grandma-san's hooch, the Hood is confronted by a wolf, disguised as a dink.[8]

"Dung lai!"[9] shouts the wolf. "Where are you going, baby-san,[10] and what have you in that doggie pack?"

"To grandma-san's hooch," replies the badly frightened Hood. "Cut me some slack,[11] Sir Charles.[12] There's only ti-ti[13] chow[14] in this pack, some motherfuckers and beans,[15] couple warm bamebas,[16] bottle of Saigon tea,[17] that's all." Despite her bold front, the Hood is shakin' 'n quakin',[18] and her pucker factor[19] is very high. She says a silent prayer: Yea, though I walk through the valley of the shadow of death, I will fear no evil; for I am the meanest motherfucker in the valley.[20] Short![21] she adds by way of amen.

"You sao!"[22] screams the wolf. Then more calmly: "Listen, cherry girl,[23] obviously you have mistaken me for some dinky dow[24] motherfucker, huh? I know you numbah fuckin' ten[25] cheap charlie,[26] so di-fucking-mau,[27] slopehead,[28] and never come this way again, or I cacadow[29] you! Bic?"[30]

"Be nice![31] You speak numbah queo, GI!"[32] counters the Hood. But before the wolf can answer, the Hood di-di's[33] on down the trail to grandma-san's hooch. Yet even as Hood runs to grandma-san's, the wolf takes a shortcut to arrive there first, whereupon he greases[34] grandma-san's ass, slips into same-same's[35] tiger stripes,[36] and climbs into her rack,[37] there to wait the imminent arrival of Hood with the bennies.[38]

The Hood arrives, knocks on the door, and to the wolf's falsetto, "Lai day,[39] motherfucker!", enters.

"Chou[40] grandma-san! Enjoyin' yer R&R?[41] I've brought you some charlie's rats!"[42] As she places the pack next to grandma-san's bed, the Hood makes a double-take. "Choi-oi,[43] you got the biggest fuckin' eyeballs I ever seen on a gook,"[44] she says.

"Big as blooper balls,"[45] answers the wolf, "but all the better to see you with."

"And your ears are maxed to the onions,"[46] comments the Hood.

"Oh yeah? And yer titties're Hong Kongs,"[47] answers the wolf, somewhat annoyed by the Hood's jocular sallies at his expense.

"Calm down, grandma-san! Here, enjoy a bameba," says the Hood, tossing the wolf a bottle of beer. The Hood pries the cap off a bottle using her eyetooth. "Chin-chin, Ho Chi Minh!"[48] says the Hood, and drinks.

"Wow! That was some John Wayne!"[49] exclaims the wolf, admiring her feat in spite of himself.

"My, grandma-san, but you have beaucoup[50] teeth," observes the Hood.

"All the better to scarf you up [51] with!" roars the wolf as he tears off his Gabby Hayes [52] and comes out of the rack.

"Eeek!" screams the Hood, "the bastard's gonna waste [53] me!"

At this point papa-san [54] comes through the door carrying his pig [55] and lets the wolf have a burst on rock 'n roll,[56] effectively blowing his shit away.[57]

"Get some!"[58] screams the Hood. "Wow, did you zap [59] that zip,[60] papa-san!"

"No sweat," comments papa-san as he reloads. "What I love are free fire zones[61] and big body counts."[62] Papa-san is a grunt[63] of few words.

NOTES

1. hooch: in this sense, a native shack of somewhat insubstantial construction (bamboo, grass, clapboard, tin, etc.). It was also a name given to any kind of temporary structure used for troop housing such as quonset huts, tents, etc. Sometimes spelled *hootch* and even *hutch*. Possibly from the Japanese *uchi*, "house."

2. vil: short for "village." Sometimes *vill*, even *ville*.

3. doggie pack: the Marine Corps name for the U.S. Army's combat field pack. "Doggie" is diminutive of "dogface," a sobriquet for an Army infantryman.

4. chop: food. The origin of this word is uncertain, but it was being used in this sense as early as 1935 in the Lingua Franca of West Africa (see *American Speech*, February 1935, p. 79). The word is widely used among U.S. troops stationed in the Far East today.

5. cees: short for combat—"C"—rations. To my knowledge, the effect of cold C rations in the diet of the ailing elderly has never been observed, and I pray it never will be.

6. grandma-san: the *-san* ending is a borrowing from the Japanese meaning "the one in charge." The habit of adding *-san* to such common English words as mama, papa, baby (see notes 10 and 54), to give them an "Oriental" sound, became widespread among U.S. service personnel stationed in the Far East during and after the years of the Japanese Occupation. It eventually became part of the patois used by Americans and Vietnamese. Many Vietnamese thought the affectation an Americanism.

7. punji: a highly sharpened wooden stake used in man-traps and *cheval-de-frise* in fortifications. They caused painful and incapacitating wounds; often they were smeared with human excrement, to hasten the process of infection. Sometimes spelled *pongi* and even *pongee*.

8. **dink:** a derogatory name for a Vietnamese. I think it reasonable that the word as it was used in Vietnam came from *dinky dow* (see note 24), reinforced by "dinky," describing a person of small stature or a thing of little value. Flexner (*I Hear America Talking*, Van Nostrand, 1976) discounts any influence from *dinky*. Both H.L. Mencken and Eric Partridge (*The American Language, Supplement One* and *A Dictionary of Slang and Unconventional English*, respectively) point out that in Australian slang *dink* has meant a Chinese since at least as early as the 1920s, but I doubt that any American soldier in Vietnam ever knew this; the Australians who served there with us simply did not have that great a linguistic impact on U.S. forces personnel. Folk etymologies attribute the word to a shortening of "rinky-dink" and a Vietnamese word meaning "a hairy man from the jungle," first used by the Viets to describe *us* (!).

9. **dung lai:** stop. From the Vietnamese *dừng lại* ("dung" is pronounced "yung" in the South Vietnamese dialect; "zung" in the Hanoi dialect; most GIs pronounced the phrase "dung lie").

10. **baby-san:** a child or young girl (see note 6).

11. **cut slack:** to ease up on or give a break to someone.

12. **Sir Charles:** The Viet Cong soldier. Here Hood has mistaken the wolf for a Viet Cong, which is natural, because in Vietnam one never knew whose side the local people were on. "Sir Charles" was always a formidable enemy, hence the term of respect, but generally the GIs referred to him simply as "Charlie or "Victor Charlie," from the phonetic alphabet for the letters *V* and *C*. The Viet Cong were mostly ethnic South Vietnamese.

13. **ti-ti:** a little. A reduplication of the Vietnamese *ti*, a little, a bit; nearly, almost. Sometimes spelled *tee-tee*. I

do not give credence to the opinion that the expression derives from the *Petit Nègre* French, *petit-petit*, "teeny bit."

14. **chow:** food. This term is very old and now standard in the U.S. Armed Forces. Flexner (ibid., note 8) thinks it comes from the Mandarin Chinese *ch'ao*, to stir, fry, cook, and Wentworth and Flexner (*Dictionary of American Slang*, Crowell, 1975) trace its use, in this sense, as far back as 1856 in California.

15. **motherfuckers and beans:** the canned beans and frankfurters that are a standard component of the Combat rations issued to the troops. This was a very unpopular meal with the troops in Vietnam, but if you're hungry enough, you'll eat anything.

16. **bamebas:** the "33" beer brewed by the *Brasseries et Glacières de l'Indochine* in Saigon and very popular throughout South Vietnam. *Ba Mươi ba* (mispronounced "ba-me-ba" by most Americans) is Vietnamese for "thirty-three." Also called *bomb-ne-bomb* and *bamidy-bam* (possibly reinforced by the fact that one could really get "bombed" on the stuff).

17. **Saigon tea:** real tea or colored water pushed by Saigon's bargirls. Early in the war (1962-63) the oft-heard refrain from those young ladies was "You buy me Saigon tea, sixty pee!" Sixty "pee," South Vietnamese piasters, amounted to a trifle less than a dollar in those days. The price of Saigon tea escalated with the warfare and the practice of pushing it in GI dives spread to all the towns and villages of South Vietnam where drinking establishments catered to American troops. *Saigon tea* eventually became synonymous with "falseness" and "cheating" (compare with note 47).

18. **shakin' 'n quakin':** afraid (see next note).

19. **pucker factor:** the degree to which one's sphincter contracts when experiencing great trepidation.

20. **the meanest motherfucker in the valley:** from the infamous "Special Forces Prayer," playing on the 23rd

Psalm of David. See *Maledicta* 4 (1980), p. 172, note 3.

21. **short:** very close to the end of one's Vietnam tour of duty (which was set at one year, give or take a few days). Military authorities noted with alarm a serious deterioration of soldiers' attitudes when they became "short," as if they really didn't care about the fucking war anymore.

22. **sao:** to lie. From the Vietnamese *xảo* "cleverness, cunning," pronounced very much like "sow," which has led many people to believe it means a repulsive, disagreeable, dishonest or stupid person. The expression was frequently used as a rejoinder by Vietnamese bargirls to the romantic importunings of their aroused (or drunken, or both) customers, as in "You sao, GI!" or, "You're lying, soldier!"

23. **cherry girl:** a virgin. It was a common joke among American soldiers in Vietnam that "the only cherry you're gonna get while you're here's the one you get in your drink."

24. **dinky dow:** crazy, insane. From the Vietnamese *điên cài đầu*, literally "crazy head," which is pronounced something like "dinky dow." As pointed out above (note 8), I think this expression contributed to the origin of the word "dink," for a Vietnamese. This expression was very popular among Vietnamese and Americans from early 1962 onward. We called one of the Vietnamese employees at the advisory detachment where I was assigned in 1962 "dink," because his favorite expression was "You dinky dow, GI!" He was probably right, of course, but we did not consider *him* very normal and he was a diminutive person, so the name seemed to fit him perfectly. *Res adjudicata?*

25. **numbah ten:** very bad, the worst; number ten. "Numbah" is a mimic on the trouble many Vietnamese have when they try to pronounce the "-ber" in "number." The system of indicating the relative worth of something (or someone) on a sliding scale of numerical value is very current in the pidgin English used by American service personnel throughout the Far East. In this system "number

one" is the best and "number ten" the worst. Frequently something or someone is described as "number ten thou(sand)" or "number one thou(sand)" to emphasize the degree of negativity. See note 32, below.

26. **cheap charlie:** a miserly, stingy person; a niggardly tipper. Where this expression came from is a mystery. Folk etymology associates it with the Chong Nam Restaurant on Hai Ba Trung Street in Saigon, which was called "Cheap Charlie's" as early as 1962—because it was cheap to eat there—and supposes that the expression entered Saigon's nightclub patois (and hence Viet-Speak in general) from Cheap Charlie's. The expression was often used in constructions such as, "You number fucking ten cheap charlie GI cocksucker!" and others, too squalid and shocking to blight the pages of this serious and scholarly journal.

27. **di-fucking-mau:** scram, beat it. From the Vietnamese *đi mau*, "go quickly." Sometimes spelled *di mau* (see note 33, below).

28. **slopehead:** a derogatory name for a Vietnamese. It was widely believed among the American troops that the Vietnamese were so stupid that their heads were pointed. This view may have been somewhat reinforced by the fact that many Vietnamese are excessively brachycephalic.

29. **cacadow:** to cut someone's throat; to kill. Sometimes rendered *cec ce dao*, I consider it very likely that the expression derives from the Vietnamese expression *cạc cai đao*, "kill the duck." "I cacadow you, GI!" was always meant facetiously, and the expression was frequently accompanied by a gesture of drawing the forefinger across the throat.

30. **bic:** to understand. From the Vietnamese *biết*, "to understand, comprehend."

31. **be nice:** a feigned expression of shock or disgust.

32. **numbah queo:** worse than "number ten" (see note 25), possibly as bad as "number twelve." Folk etymology attributes the origin of the term *queo* to the difficulty Viet-

namese have in pronouncing the number twelve in English.

33. **di-di:** a reduplication of the Vietnamese *đi*, "to go." As noted in 27, the degree of speed with which one desires to depart is indicated by the addition of certain modals to the verb. Author Joe Haldeman (*War Year*, Pocket Books, 1972, p. 94) explained it very succinctly when he wrote: "'di di' means 'get outa here' and 'di di mao' means 'get the *fuck* outa here.'"

34. **grease:** to kill. Widely used in Vietnam, but I am ignorant of its etymology. The Vietnam War seems to have spawned a large number of euphemisms for death and killing. Among these were *to blow away, burn, buy it, buy the farm, ding, dust, grease, hose down, to be K.I.A.* (killed in action), *to light up, massage, use up, waste, wax, zap.*

35. **same-same:** just like; same as; that is, grandma's. This expression has been very popular in GI pidgin since at least as early as 1955 (see Norman, *American Speech*, May 1956, pp. 107-112).

36. **tiger stripes:** a jungle uniform camouflaged with alternating patches of light and dark colors.

37. **rack:** bed. Most military beds have the same effect upon one's ability to sleep as spending the night on a Medieval torture instrument.

38. **bennies:** benefits, as used here. This expression comes from the trite encomiums of recruiting sergeants when they extoll the benefits of a military career.

39. **lai day:** come here. From the Vietnamese *lại đây*, "to come here."

40. **chou:** greetings, hello. From the Vietnamese *chào*, "greetings." Pronounced somewhere between "chow" and "meow." Note similarity with Italian *ciao* "hello," "good-bye."

41. **R&R:** Rest and Recuperation leave; time off from the war, usually at some spot outside Vietnam to which soldiers were provided government transportation (places such as Hong Kong, Singapore, Bangkok, Sydney, etc.).

42. **charlie's rats:** "C"—"charlie" in the phonetic alphabet—rations (see note 5).

43. **choi-oi:** Alas! Good heavens! From the Vietnamese *chao ôi*, which was pronounced by Americans as "choi-oi(oy)."

44. **gook:** a derogatory name for any oriental person. This is a very old expression in the U.S. Armed Forces, possibly dating from the years of the Philippine Pacification (1898-1913) when the insurrectionists were referred to as *gugus*, hence a derogatory name for all Filipinos. The term gained wide acceptance in WW II and Korea, especially Korea, where the Korean word *kuk*, "nationality" (pronounced "kook") is used in such combinations as *Chungkuk* (Chinese), *Hankuk* (Koreans) and *Mykuk* (Americans). The derogatory connotation of this word is reinforced by comparisons with goo, grease, dirt, slime, gobbledygook (which is the way most GIs think oriental languages sound).

45. **blooper balls:** 40-mm grenades fired from the M-79 grenade launcher (known as a *blooper, blooker, chunker,* and *thump gun*, because of the sounds it makes when fired).

46. **maxed to the onions:** very large. A neologism; I do not know the origin of this expression. It appears to be a nonce expression that was current in the 1970s.

47. **Hong Kong:** something cheap, false; an imitation. From the padded brassières manufactured in Hong Kong and worn by Vietnamese ladies, many of whom are under-endowed in the chest. By extension (no pun intended) the term *Hong Kong* came to mean anything that was cheaply made or falsely represented. An illustration of how this expression was used concerns a certain Navy lieutenant commander who told me that as he sat in a Saigon bistro, he playfully squeezed a young barmaid's ample bosom and asked her, facetiously, "You Hong Kong?" Far from affronted, the brazen lady placed her hand on his penis, squeezed, and asked "*You* Hong Kong?"

48. **Chin-chin Ho Chi Minh:** a toast popular among Saigon's bargirls during the "middle years" of the Vietnam War (ca 1966-1969). Ostensibly a mockery of Ho Chi Minh's plans to subjugate South Vietnam, I've always wondered if the expression did not belie an unconscious desire for insurance, "just in case." "Chin-chin" comes from the Mandarin Chinese *ts'ing-ts-ing*, "please-please," and has been a popular toasting expression in Western Europe for many years. Many Vietnamese thought the expression American in origin, that is, *chin-chin*. The first time I ever heard it used was in Saigon in March 1962.

49. **John Wayne:** a heroic or very macho deed (such as pulling grenade pins with your eyetooth); one who does heroic or macho deeds; the hard way to do things ("John Wayning it"); a can opener issued with C rations (also called a P-38). After the late John Wayne, who excelled in the portrayal of strong, heroic men of action. Author Tom Suddick (*A Few Good Men*, Avon Books, 1978, p. 18) put it very well when he wrote, "Have you ever thought about how many ways 'John Wayne' can be used? I mean, linguistically speaking, it's almost as versatile a word as 'fuck.'"

50. **beaucoup:** many, much. Vietnam was a French colony for many years, and this word was a linguistic survival from those days.

51. **scarf up:** to eat. A borrowing from the general American slang lexicon, but widely used among U.S. troops in South Vietnam.

52. **Gabby Hayes:** a floppy narrow-brim bush hat issued to soldiers in Vietnam, reminiscent of the one worn by the character actor who played the role of "Gabby" in the old "Roy Rogers" TV Western series.

53. **waste:** to kill. See note 34 for synonyms.

54. **papa-san:** any old man. See note 6.

55. **pig:** any firearm that can be carried and used by an individual soldier.

56. **rock 'n roll:** the full automatic setting on the M-16 rifle, possibly from the sensation of rocking and rolling when the weapon is fired fully automatic.

57. **blow away:** to kill. See note 34 for synonyms.

58. **get some:** literally, "kill some for me." This phrase was frequently heard among U.S. troops in Vietnam as they would watch a distant firefight, bombing raid or artillery firing mission. It is wildly exciting, even cathartic, to watch the *other* guy get the shit pounded out of him.

59. **zap:** to kill. See note 34 for synonyms.

60. **zip:** a derogatory name for a Vietnamese. From the widely held view among Americans in Vietnam that the natives were zeros, not fully human, worthless.

61. **free fire zones:** areas inside South Vietnam declared fully in the control of the enemy where anything and everything could be freely shot to hell, whether or not it could shoot back.

62. **body counts:** the much maligned method of evaluating the success of military engagements by counting the bodies (or body parts) left on the battlefield by the enemy. Commanders desiring to minimize their own losses have been known to inflate enemy body counts.

63. **grunt:** another name for an infantryman. Evidence seems to indicate that the term was coined by Marine aviators in the late 1950s or early 1960s. It is now used by all the Armed Services. Although probably derogatory to begin with (*grunt* = shit), infantrymen are extremely proud of the sobriquet (see *Maledicta* 4, p. 168).

▲ Many West Germans, angered by the unusually cold and wet summer of 1980, **sent insulting postcards** to the weather bureau. (*New York Times* Service, 28 July 1980)

▲ As late as the 1930s, there was a small sign backstage in each legitimate theater and vaudeville house outside New York City, reading: THE WORDS "HELL" AND "DAMN", AND THE NAME OF THE DEITY, ARE NOT TO BE PRONOUNCED ON THIS STAGE. (G. Legman, Letter to the Editor, 23 Aug. 1980)

Taxonomic Pornithology
Rules for the Naming of Egregious and Obscene Birds

Douglas Lindsey

Synthetic pornithology is the development of avian labels to describe varieties of human appearance and behavior. The obligate brevity of ornithologic nomenclature suggests relationship with both the one-liner and the pun, but these mechanisms do not adequately explain the range of possibilities of synthetic ornithology as a form of humor.

Labeling a person as a bird is not new. All academicians are familiar with the pejorative labeling of a visiting lecturer as a **turkey**, and more than a few of us have, on occasion, legitimately earned the designation. Tucson, by virtue of its far southern location in the Great American Desert, is the destination in winter of great flocks of migrating **snowbirds**, for which more precise speciation is possible. The **greater greenbacked snowbird** is enthusiastically welcomed as a "winter guest." The **lesser sooty snowbird**, on the other hand, is regarded as a pest. Euphemistically labeled as a "transient" (we try, with scant success, to encourage it to move north to Phoenix or west to Los Angeles), it befouls the shrubbery in Armory Park, clutters the lobby of the main post office with its queues before the General Delivery window, and roosts at night around campfires along the tracks of the Southern Pacific Railroad. The **lesser sooty snowbird** is accompanied by the **common stench**, always the **lesser stench**, and sometimes the **greater stench** as well.

The serious and systematic recording of collections of synthetic ornithologic species is a hobby of regrettably few devotees, and I see little prospect for a boom in the field. Perhaps the potential for proliferation of enthusiasts is greater in the field of taxonomic pornithology, a subset within synthetic ornithology which permits the venting of a pornithologic bent while offering immunity against accusation of public flatus in polite company. Provided, of course, that such verbal farting is accomplished in accordance with the recognized rules of a creative scholarly endeavor.

I will outline for you the rules of legitimate taxonomic pornithology in order to protect you from irresponsible criticism, even though I realize that taxonomic pornithology can, indeed, be practiced as a solitary vice for your own amusement, with no need for public utterance whatsoever; or it can be practiced in privy, compatible groups, where the interpersonal stimulation and instigation can be expected to lead to mutual satisfaction.

The first basic rule of taxonomic pornithology is: *it's got to sound like a bird.* You can give it a bird's name, literally, or a bird's name which is twisted slightly or punned. You can make it a bird by using avian-specific anatomy, or avian-specific functional nomenclature. You can get away with many designations which are bird-related, but not avian-specific. And when you get rolling, you can make derivations which are ornithologic only by association and context. Which brings up the second basic rule of taxonomic pornithology: *if it passes for a bird, it is.* The risk of overstretching the immunity from obscenity is your own. If you provided an adequate context, and it flies, it's a bird. If it doesn't fly, you are stuck with mouthing dirty words.

An example of the use of legitimate bird names is the **perpetual grouse**. A takeoff from the **prothonotary warbler**, which figured heavily in the Alger Hiss/Whitaker

Chambers affair, is the **penitentiary warbler**, also known as the **stool pigeon**. A medical example is the **intertriginous thrush**. But the archetypical example of the technique is the **extramarital lark**.

Tweaking the bird name just a little offers more possibilities. The **ruffled spouse** is often found in association with the **extramarital lark**. The **great American craven** proliferated enormously during the war in Viet Nam—to such numbers that large flocks migrated to Canada. The **California condom**, once thought to be near extinction as the result of advances in steroid chemistry, is now making a comeback as result of the threats induced by herpes and Acquired Immune Deficiency Syndrome (AIDS).

The door is open. If there is a *junco*, there is a **junkie**. If there is *cardinal*, there is **venial**. If there is a *phoebe*, there is a **feelie** and a **freebie**. If there is a *curlew*, there is a **curfew**. If there is a *barred avocet*, there must be a **disbarred advocate**. There are *buzzards* and *bustards*: surely there must be **bastards**, and the **yellow-bellied bastard** is one of my earliest and most faithfully recurring species.

In terms of avian-specific anatomy, my base type is the **buff-tinted due-bill**. Pornithologic? Of course. Bad enough that the scoundrel is dunning me for his ill-gotten gains; he is doing it on *off-color, laid* paper! More innocuous is **Durante's grossbeak**, from which we can develop **de Bergerac's proboscis**. But my favorite is the **right-winged sanctimoner**, or **Falwell's phallusy**. A **phallusy** is the public claim to potency and prowess which does not exist. A prime example is the man who stuffs two Kotex into the crotch of his bathing trunks to draw incredulous stares from the babes at the beach.

Anatomical terms which are not avian-specific require a little more caution. After all, there are non-avian species which can be described in their own right as full-breasted, sharp-clawed, and twitchy-tailed. But the **pearl-throated**

dowager will pass (there is a bird known as the *dowitcher*), as will the **mink-breasted Yentl**, the **bald gay**, and the **red-nosed lush**. The **three-toed American chicken** is synonymous with the **great American craven**, but so named for the footprint which he displayed in justification of his cry of conscientious aversion to wading through the jungles of Viet Nam and getting shot at.

Many legitimate avian species are labeled by particular function or behavior. If there is a *gnatcatcher*, there is surely a **nitpicker**. If there is a *roadrunner*, there must be a **streetwalker**. A good example of functional identification with birds is the **accidental flycatcher**, also known as the **impaled prepuce** or the **zippered thatch**.

There is a bird known as the *wandering tattler* which gives rise to the **village gossipmonger** and the **suburban fink**. The **all-night bed-thrasher** warms many hearts, two at a time. If there is a *white wagtail*, there must be a **black wagtail** and a **yellow wagtail**. The last implies oriental origin, so it may be called the **transverse snatch**. There is, indeed, a bird known as the *white-collared seedeater*, which translates to the **executive gay**. There is a *greater frigate bird*: why not a **lesser upyurass**?

Incidentally, the adjectives that ornithologists use are amusing in their own right. There are birds which are *fulvous*, *ferruginous*, and *flammulated*. Another legitimate ornithologic adjective is *frugiverous*, meaning "fruit-eating," which leads to the **frugiverous reciprocating gay**, implying an all-male 69.

Let us note some examples of how far out we can stretch and distort a few common and uncommon birds.

There is a Mexican bird, little known to most of you, named the *copper trogon*, from which we can deduce the **pink-ribbed Trojan** and the **rubber Ramses**. For those of you who are not from the western side of the Atlantic, I might explain that *Trojan* and *Ramses* are popular brands of condoms in the United States.

The *robin* is a common bird, but I have been able to make little of it.* The **hooded robin** comes to mind. Probably extinct now, but occasionally sighted of yore in Nottingham Forest. Hardly pornithologic, though there were some delightfully salacious obliquities in the lines of the pilot of an abortive television series. But **cradle robin** offers some opportunities: **Nabakov's Lolita** and **Polanski's nemesis**. **Cradle robin** is a species of global distribution—I remember from my youth some most exciting specimens of what was called **San Quentin quail**—but it seems to have dropped from view in Sweden since the age of consent was lowered to twelve.

The *swallow* provides much food for thought. Physicians and many patients are quite familiar with the **barium swallow**. Californians get very excited each year when the **Cappuccino swallow** returns to the mission of San Juan Cappuccino. Since this swallow always returns, we could call it the **regurgitant swallow**, but that would unnecessarily offend aficionados of Cappuccino. There is a real bird known as the *violet green swallow*, certainly a nauseating combination, perhaps to be labeled the **imminent barf**. There is a little hummingbird which is also purple and green; surely it can be labeled the **regurgitant sip**.

And then, or course, there is the **deep-throated swallow**, known also as the **plum-headed gag** or **common puke**. For the ladies who perhaps feel put upon in such matters, I offer the **avid busheater**, the **long-billed muff-diver**, the **cunning lingus**, and for those whose tastes in the matter are utterly feminine, the **Lapland gull**. But my favorite in this group is the **limber-tongued gash hawk**.

Of course, if one is serious about ornithology or pornithology one needs a "field guide"—how to identify the species if you don't have it in your grubby little hand, or in your bush. Let me tell you how to spot the **limber-**

---

*Editor's Note: The robin is Wisconsin's State Bird. Its Latin name is *Turdus migratorius.*

tongued gash hawk. He hangs out in the singles bar. He comes early, but never stays late. He comes alone, but never leaves alone. He sits at the little table in the corner, where he can look out over the whole room. He orders a huge pitcher of beer, from which he drinks, in single gulps, spaced at long intervals. Most of the time he just sits there, licking the foam from his eyebrows. His favorite beer? *Slits*.

Another bird familiar to, and beloved by almost all of you, is the *cock*. Male homosexuals think there is absolutely nothing finer than the **cock**. Virtually all admitted and practicing heterosexuals think highly of the **cock**, too. And in certain forms, the **cock** is esteemed by the lesbian. Take the **many-splintered woodcock**. Few would take it, willingly, even though it featured heavily in the romantic novel *Love is a Many-splintered Thing*. But how about the **burnished woodcock**, also known as the **mahogany dildo**?

A minor variety, but worth some discussion, is the **matutinal peecock**, also known as the **early-morning hard** or **uriniferous cock**. Morphologically it is identical with the familiar **erogenate cock**; in fact, in museum specimens—skinned and dried—the two are indistinguishable. Behaviorally they are quite different. The **erogenate cock** struts proudly during the pre-mating ritual. The **matutinal peecock** is shy, almost secretive, sometimes recognizable only by the tenting of its cover. You seldom get to examine one closely unless you have a domesticated specimen. It often runs away when it is uncovered; you might even say that it disappears when it is flushed. This accounts for an alternate nomenclature, the **fugacious phallus**. *Fugacious* means "fleeting." I would not know that, except that as a physician, I am sometimes called upon to manage cases of *proctalgia fugax*, literally translated as "a fleeting pain in the ass," which is precisely and entirely all that we know about the condition.

Of course there are a few of the species of **cock** which,

like myself, work night shifts and sleep in the daytime. This is the **vespertine peecock** which, on occasion, can be confused with the **great horny owl**.

Also familiar to you are *tits* and *boobs*. I read an article once, in that prestigious scientific journal *Nature*, on the feeding habits of *great tits*—nutritional requirements and food intake. This has confused me; I had always thought it was the other way round. Incidentally, I have never quite understood the alleged erogenous importance of size in **great tits**. It seems that simply quoting the numbers *38-27-35* is supposed to be an instant turn-on. More important, I think, is form, feel and flavor. There are **silicone tits**; their flavor is poor.

Boobies are closely related to **tits**. The corollary to the *great tits* is the **saddle-bag booby**, usually observed in the **shrouded** variety. The **lesser shrouded booby** is also known as the **cross-your-heart bra**, and the **least shrouded booby** is also known as **Frederick's pastie**.

Finally, there is a group of birds known as the *ani*. If you will permit me the presumption that the singular of *ani* is *anus*, this opens up other avenues for exploration. There is the **patulous anus**, and the **petulant anus**. There is the **pendulous anus**, also known as the **prolapsed pile**. And, of course, there is the **fiery-red anus**, known also as the **tabasco twat**, **el ano salsado**, or simply the **Mexican heartburn**.

Let me encourage you to take up the hobby of taxonomic pornithology. If you think I have exhausted the possibilities, think again. Get hold of a copy of *Mrs. Byrne's Dictionary of Unusual, Obscure, and Preposterous Words*. Find an unusual adjective, and then hang it on a bird. For example, the **obvallate fink** is synonymous with the **penitentiary warbler**. Find an unusual noun, and use it. The word *rantallion* is British slang for a man whose balls hang lower than his pecker. Obviously, then, there are *two* avian species: the **short-dinked rantallion**, and the **big-knockered rantallion**. Find both noun and adjective. The **jubate merkin** is a female pudendum with hair like a horse's mane. The **irrumant agomphyx** is the nice little old lady—the *cute* nice little old lady—who takes her teeth out before she goes down on you. When you return the favor, you can identify the **poliotic pubis**, also known as the **mottled muff**, the **bespotted beaver**, or the **salt-and-pepper snatch**. And how about the **preprandial pallion**, literally translated as "a little piece before lunch," also known as the **quickie**?

What is the meaning of all this pornithology? One of the Justices of the Supreme Court of the United States once commented that if pornography had any redeeming virtue at all, he would give it the protection of freedom of the press. Taxonomic pornithology does have a redeeming virtue. Sit in the middle seat of an Aer Lingus wide-bodied jet. Stare up at the ceiling, and stare all around you, looking for pornithologic species. Move your lips slowly while naming species, without uttering a sound. Then smile, giggle, and occasionally break out in hearty laughter. Soon the flight attendant will find other seats for the passengers on your right and left, and you can stretch out and sleep, or continue to amuse yourself without abusing yourself, all the way across the Atlantic.

Why did the gay rooster cross the basketball court?
—*Because he heard that the referee was blowing fowls.*

What's the difference between a garbage can and a Tennessee coed?
—*A garbage can gets taken out once a week.*

How do the Tennessee coeds discourage peeping toms?
—*They leave their shades up.*

Common Patient-Directed Pejoratives Used by Medical Personnel

C. J. Scheiner

All professions have a slang which serves to convey a large amount of information or an entire situation in a shorthand form. Negative feelings or situations can be expressed verbally, and often very colorfully, through the use of pejoratives which, if they are incorporated into a professional slang, become part of a semi-secret vocabulary that reinforces a sense of solidarity and separation from others not of the particular profession.

Two conditions anger physicians and medical personnel in particular: *(1)* patients who do not follow medical advice, and *(2)* patients who do not respond as expected to medical therapy. The former may be considered a defiance of authority, while the latter is a reminder of the limitations of the medical practitioner.

The following is a short list of commonly encountered pejoratives directed against patients, collected from oral use in a large hospital in New York, from 1976 to 1978. The list does not include terms as commonly used by non-medical personnel, for example *stupid* or *creep,* nor does it include pejoratives that simply incorporate medically related terms, e.g., *spineless* or *shithead.* This study is not in any way exhaustive, and does not include many terms used possibly in various specialty areas of this particular hospital, and certainly not all the terms used in various hospitals in or outside of New York.

Botanist see **Veterinarian**

What's the difference between a proctologist and a bartender?
— *A proctologist takes care of only one asshole at a time.*

What's a proctoscope?
— *A long tube with an asshole at each end.*

Crock   a patient who medically abuses himself, often with alcohol. Either short for "crock of shit" or from "crocked" = drunk.

Dispo   a patient admitted to the hospital with no real medical problem other than being unable to care for himself/herself in his/her present circumstances. Short for "**dispo**sition problem."

Ethanolic   an alcoholic.

F.O.S.   abbreviation for "full of shit." 1: a severely constipated patient, often impacted with months of unpassed feces. 2: a patient who lies to gain medically unnecessary drugs.

Fruit Salad   a group of stroke patients, all totally unable to care for themselves. See **Vegetable**.

Geologist   see **Veterinarian**

Gork   a mentally deficient patient, either congenitally, secondary to chronic drug or alcohol abuse, or following a cerebral contusion or bleed. Also, "to heavily sedate."

Gorked Out   semi-comatose.

Gun and Rifle Club   a trauma ward to which stabbing and gunshot victims are admitted.

Hotdog   a flamboyant or bizarre patient, usually with psychiatric problems.

H.Y.S.   abbreviation for "**h**ysterical."

International House of Pancakes   a neurology ward occupied by patients, often stroke victims, all of whom babble in a different language.

Loxed   a decreased state of consciousness, usually following a cardiac or respiratory arrest. Contraction for "lack of oxygen." Also, "loxed out."

No Squash   a condition of irreparable brain damage, most often from trauma, intracranial hemorrhage, drug abuse, or prolonged anoxia; see **Vegetable Garden**.

O.D.   abbreviation for "overdose." A particularly despised patient, as the cause of this malady is self-induced.

Pits   the medical screening area of a hospital, particularly hated by physicians because of the enormous amounts of insignificant medical maladies that must be treated there in a hospital setting. Also known as the **Screaming Area**.

P.M.D. abbreviation for "private medical doctor." A physician who refers his apparently ill patients to the hospital Emergency Room rather than diagnose and treat them himself. This is one of the few pejoratives directed at a member of the professional group.

P.O.S. abbreviation for "piece of shit." A general term for patients medically ill because of their own failure to care for themselves (most often alcoholics).

Potato Patch see **Vegetable Garden**

P.P. abbreviation for "professional patient." A person who appears regularly, either daily or weekly, at the Emergency Room for trivial complaints such as the refill of innocuous medicines or the treatment of chronic symptoms that are never present at the time of examination.

P.P.P. abbreviation for "piss poor protoplasm." A debilitated patient, often requiring surgery, who needs extensive medical treatment, including transfusions, before he is able to undergo definitive therapy.

Quack a patient who fakes symptoms to gain unnecessary hospitalization or drugs.

Rose Garden see **Vegetable Garden**

Saturday Night Special a patient, usually an alcoholic, who has spent his money, and comes to the hospital on the weekend looking for a meal and a place to stay.

Schizo short for "**schizo**phrenic." Any mentally abnormal patient.

Screamer a hysterical patient.

Screaming Area see **Pits**

Scut menial medical procedures that must be carried out, usually relegated to the least senior member of the medical team. Also, any patient held in extremely low esteem.

SHPOS acronym for "sub-human piece of shit." A chronic **P.O.S.** A critically ill patient who, after intensive medical care and rehabilitation, fails to follow medical instructions, and is readmitted to the hospital in his previous critical condition.

Stage Mother an adult who coaches younger patients as to their alleged symptoms, and generally states what medical tests and procedures are necessary.

Stroked Out in a state of decreased consciousness and muscular ability following a cerebral bleed.

Subway Rider a patient who comes to the Emergency Room with minor or non-existing medical complaints as a means to getting free subway fare home.

Turkey a patient with a trivial medical complaint.

Two Carbon Abuser An alcoholic. From the chemical formula for alcohol, C_2H_6O (C_2 = 2 carbon atoms).

Vegetable a neurologically depressed patient, usually as result of a stroke, who is totally unable to care for himself. Also called **potato, carrot, cucumber,** or the name of any other specific vegetable or plant.

Vegetable Garden a group of unconscious or semi-conscious patients. Also known as **Rose Garden, Potato Patch,** etc.

Veterinarian a physician who considers his patients of less than human intelligence. Related terms: **Botanist**: an M.D. with patients of less than animal intelligence; and **Geologist**: an M.D. with patients of absolutely no intelligence.

Water the Garden to change the intravenous bottles that serve as the sole source of nourishment for severely neurologically impaired patients.

Editor's Note: As reported in the *Süddeutsche Zeitung* (Germany) of 19 April 1978, page 13, verbal abuse of the patients by physicians also exists in Germany. Professor Dr. Albert Göb, head of the spastics center in Munich, is involved in a major scandal caused in part by his continuous verbal attacks on the 300 handicapped youths at the center. He calls them *Deppen* (dopes), *Idioten* (idiots), *blöde Deppen* (stupid idiots), *Kartoffelköpfe* (potatoheads), and *Dummköpfe* (dumbheads).

What's a committee?
—*A life form with six or more legs and no brains.*

What goes "ha-ha-ha-ha THUMP"?
—*A leper laughing his head off.*

Not Sticks and Stones, But Names
More Medical Pejoratives

Lois Monteiro

In a recent issue of *Maledicta*, C. J. Scheiner[1] presented a list of patient-directed pejorative terms, collected from oral use by the personnel of a large New York hospital. His list included terms related to patients, to places in the hospital, and to procedures performed upon patients. Although Scheiner does not cite any other studies of medical language, there have been a few previously published lists that have included some of the terms Scheiner collected, as well as other terms, some of which are pejorative. These collections are reviewed below, along with some new words that I have collected from nurses in New England Hospitals.

Peter Hukill,[2] writing on the "Argot, Slang and Cant" in medical language, included these pejorative terms among his longer list of general terms:

Crock: A patient who complains continually of multiple symptoms, many of which are either imaginary or of psychic origin. Scheiner defines *crock* as a patient who medically abuses himself, often with alcohol.
Gas Passer: An anesthetist.
Head Shrinker: A psychiatrist. He also lists **Spook** and **Wig Picker** for psychiatrist.
Hot Belly: An acute condition of the abdomen for which immediate surgical intervention is indicated.
Knife Happy: An overeager surgeon.
Lunger: A patient with chronic lung disease.
Pill Pusher: A specialist in internal medicine.

What's a macho WASP?
— *One who jogs home after getting a vasectomy.*

Plumber: A urologist.

Stroker: A patient suffering from a cerebrovascular accident or stroke. Scheiner lists *stroked out* with a similar definition.

Turkey: A patient who has been medically mishandled. Scheiner defines a *turkey* as a patient with a trivial medical complaint.

A study of student nurses by Olesen and Whittaker[3] reported the use of the words "gung-ho" and "red hot" as derogatory remarks directed at those student nurses who were overly committed and dedicated to their work or study.

Philip Kolin[4] listed these pejoratives along with a number of other items from nursing language:

Monkey Jacket: A hospital garment worn as pajamas by patients.

Dirty Bed: A bed for patients who have pneumonia or any other infectious disease.

Rear Admiral: A proctologist or a proctoscopic exam of the rectum.

Pinky Cheater: A condom-like covering a physician uses on his finger when he examines a patient's rectum.

Running Off: Diarrhea.

Pink Puffer: A thin patient suffering from emphysema. Overweight ones are called **Blue Bloaters**.

Rose: A comatose patient, expected to die. **Rose Room:** Room for comatose patients. Scheiner lists *Rose Garden* as a group of unconscious patients.

Gas Passer: An anesthetist.

Spaced Out *or* **Gorked:** Stupefied from anesthesia. Scheiner lists *gorked* as semi-comatose.

Alkie: An alcoholic.

Zap [a patient]: To give an electroshock treatment to someone.

Gomer: A long-term care patient usually sent to a nursing home.

Further medical terms were reported by Barbara Pinson[5] in her "Doctor, There's a Gomer in the Pit." Pinson includes *gomer, turkey, gorked, pit,* and *vegetable garden* listed above or in Scheiner. In addition, she reports the following derisive terms:

Boxed: Refers to a patient's death. "I just boxed the carcinoma patient."

Hit: The process by which a resident receives his patients. Patients are distributed to residents as they are admitted; each patient is a "hit."

Shpos: A more caustic term for *gomer*; letters are an acronym for "*s*ub-*h*uman *p*iece *o*f *s*hit."

Toad: Synonym for *gomer*; "a trashy old alcoholic derelict."

SICU (pronounced "Sick-you"): From *S*urgical *I*ntensive *C*are *U*nit.

Strike Out: A patient who is *gorked* or *boxed*.

The term *gomer* that was reported both by Kolin and by Pinson was the subject of an article by Victoria George and Alan Dundes.[6] They examined the term as a figure of folk speech among persons in "scientific" non-folkloric occupations. In addition to providing an analysis of the origin of the term *gomer* and a discussion of its pervasiveness in the San Francisco area, the authors make note of the terms *gork*, *turkey* and *vegetable* and give some other derisive terms that can be added to Scheiner's collection:

Blade: A surgeon.

Grume: A filthy *gomer*.

Lizard: A near-synonym for *gomer*; a physically dirty patient with scaly skin

Reeker: A dirty patient with a strong disagreeable body odor.

Trainwreck: A very sick patient who has several medical problems simultaneously and is usally comatose.

The list of derisive terms that follows has not been previously published. These are terms that I have collected from nurses and hospital personnel in the New England area over the past decade:

Andy Gump: A surgical operation for cancer of the jaw; the mandible is removed and the patient appears to have no chin (like the comic strip character).

Basket Case: A patient with multiple injuries.

D Day (Ducolax Day): The day Ducolax suppositories are given. Used at a particular Veteran's hospital where there is a routine day to give suppositories to the bed-ridden patients.

Dirty Case: An operation in which an infection is found.

Dirty Girl: A nurse who remains in the operating room during surgery. Does not assist at the operating table, nor does she wear a sterile gown. Rather, this person remains free to bring additional supplies, etc.

Dirty Room: Operating room in which there has been surgery during which an infection has been found. The room must be washed thoroughly and disinfected before being used again.

Dusting and Cleaning: Slang for *D & C* (dialation and curettage), a surgical operation to scrape out or clean the uterus.

Duck: A urinal for male patients.

Finger Wave: A rectal examination.

Gobbler: Synonym for *turkey* (a patient with a trivial complaint).

Hospitalitis: Irritability, crankiness displayed by patients following an extended hospital stay.

Hospitalized: A patient who is demanding and wise to the ways of hospital routine.

Pan the patients: To pass out bedpans.

Peri Care: Cleaning the vulva after delivery.

Pot: A patient who complains a great deal without legitimate reason for complaint: another name for *crock* or *turkey*.

P.I.D.: A *p*elvic *i*nflamatory *d*isease; code name for gonorrhea.

Probie: A probationer; a student nurse in the first six months of training. Usually subject of jokes about the naive initiate.

Quad: A quadraplegic; a person with all four limbs paralyzed.

Rosebud: The opening of the intestine on the abdomen following a colostomy or ileostomy. It is a pink, mucuous tissue mass about one inch across.

Seizure Stick: A padded tongue depressor to keep the mouth open during convulsion. Also called a **mouth gag.**

Stirrups: Supports holding the female patient's legs spread for delivery or surgery on the genital area; cf. "in the saddle" as a term for sexual intercourse.

Three H Enema: An aggressive enema: "*H*igh, *H*ot and a *H*ell of a Lot" (also noted in George & Dundes).

Welcome Sleeves: Firm material wrapped around a child's arms to prevent his bending his elbows to touch his head or face. The arms are held straight and outspread in a "welcoming" position.

I have also collected some pejorative terms for medical specialities to add to *Plumber, Rear Admiral* and *Gas Passer* reported above in the 1961 Hukill article. These are:

Baby Catcher: An obstetrician.
Butcher: A surgeon.
Carpenter: An orthopedist; "strong as a horse and twice as smart."
Comprehensive Physician: A proctologist, because he looks at the *hole* person; proctologists see their patients as a *hole*.
Cutting Doctor: A surgeon.
Guessing Doctor: An internist.
Mack-the-Knife: A surgeon.
Meat Cutter: A surgeon.
Pill Pusher: An internist; also, a pharmacist.
Saw Bones: A surgeon.
Skin Flicks: Slides used by dermatologists to show disease conditions at teaching rounds.
Skin Game: Dermatology.
Tooth Carpenter: A dentist.

The range and number of these terms suggests the extensiveness of verbal aggression towards patients among medical personnel. These terms are all used "backstage," never in the presence of a conscious patient. They may serve, as Scheiner and George & Dundes suggest, to relieve some of the tension and stress of dealing with very sick persons. At any rate, they are ample evidence of the failure of "affective neutrality" or detached concern that theorists of medical sociology have attributed to the profession of medicine. Medical personnel do have their verbal ways of getting back at patients.

REFERENCES

[1] C. J. Scheiner, "Common Patient-Directed Pejoratives Used by Medical Personnel," *Maledicta* II (1978), 67-70.

[2] Peter Hukill, "The Spoken Language of Medicine: Argot, Slang, Cant," *American Speech* 36 (May, 1961), 145-148.

[3] Virginia Olesen and Elvi Whittaker, "Conditions Under Which College Students Borrow, Use, and Alter Slang," *American Speech* 43 (October, 1968), 222-228.

[4] Philip Kolin, "The Language of Nursing," *American Speech* 48 (Fall-Winter, 1973), 192-210.

[5] Barbara Pinson, "Language: Doctor, There's a Gomer in the Pit," *Philadelphia Magazine* (November, 1977), 145-151.

[6] Victoria George and Alan Dundes, "The Gomer," *Journal of American Folklore* 91 (Jan.-March, 1978), 568-581.

A Recipe for All Seasons
BANANA BREAD
(Serves 2)

4 Laughing Eyes	*2 Milk Containers*
4 Loving Arms	*1 Fur-lined Mixing Bowl*
2 Well-shaped Legs	*1 Banana and 2 Nuts*

Method: Looking into laughing eyes, spread well-shaped legs slowly. Squeeze and massage milk containers very gently, until fur-lined mixing bowl is well greased. Check frequently with middle finger. Add banana and gently work in and out until well creamed. Cover with nuts and sigh with relief. Bread is done when banana becomes soft. Be sure to wash mixing utensils, and don't lick the bowl.

Note: If bread rises, leave town.

Scram!
Or, 101 Ways to Sack Your Lover

Laurence E. Seits and Robert M. Schumacher

One of the more fruitful places to study maledicta, and one still largely untapped, is the American school. Some studies, such as Bob Alexander's study of "Male and Female Rest Room Graffiti" and Sandra McCosh's "Aggression in Children's Jokes," have begun to mine this vein of verbal aggression.

That youth should prove rich in maledicta should not be surprising. Certain characteristics of this age group, such as youthfully creative minds, lack of social graces and training, and frankness, enable young people to be richly insulting.

In 1978, the authors, a college instructor of a Freshman English Composition course at Plano (Illinois) High School and a senior student at that school, undertook the collection and study of insulting terms which were being used by high school students at several local high schools. The specific terms studied were those used to tell an unwanted peer to depart or leave a group. More specifically, consider this hypothetical situation: a clique of four high school male students is discussing the previous Friday night's revels. A fifth male, an intruder or outsider, enters the group to join or overhear the private conversation. The original clique of four wishes the newcomer to leave. Endemic in American youth is the ability for unnecessary cruelty. Rather than telling the newcomer straightforwardly, "Please leave, this is none of your business," a member of the clique may use an insult in asking the newcomer to leave: "Why don't you make like a fart and blow away!" Of course, this genre may also be used to reject an unwanted lover.

What do you call a Mexican with a vasectomy?
— *Dry Martinez.*

This, then, is the heretofore unstudied and unnamed type of maledicta that we observed. We do not know how widespread this type of insult is but suspect that these insulting requests are virtually universal in American schools. In the absence of a better term, we have chosen to label such imperatives for departure, i. e., "Make like horseshit and hit the trail!" as *exvitations*, the opposite of *in*vitations. Although our study thus far has focused on requests for departure, imperatives of a similar form or structure also exist which make a strong and insulting request for other kinds of actions. For example, a strong request to cease speaking: "Make like a light switch and click off!" or "Make like a suppository and cram it!" Others include a request to be seated, "Make like a fish and perch!" or "Make like a chicken and roost!" For a request for action, "Make like a doctor and operate!", "Make like a mortician and undertake!" or "Make like a mother and labor!" For a strong request to stand up: "Make like the sun and rise!" The ultimate request to leave is the request to die. For example, "Make like a doornail and die!", "Make like a mule and kick the bucket!", "Make like a toad and croak!" or "Make like a thought and perish!" Almost every example of this genre that we collected was indeed similaic. Thus, for this larger group we are proposing the generic term *similimperatives*, an obvious portmanteau coinage combining *simile* and *imperative*.

Listed below are some examples of the subgroup of *exvitations* found in one relatively small area of northeast Illinois used by high school students during the early months of 1978. They have been listed and classified here using Aman's taxonomy (*Maledicta*, I/2:317-22).

HUMAN
Make like a boy scout and decamp!
  ... a cowboy and mosey along!
  ... a dragster and lay rubber!
  ... a hockey player and get the puck out of here!
  ... a hotel guest and check out!

... an infant and toddle along!
... a lady at a garage sale and bye-bye! [buy, buy]
... a mechanic and re-tire!
... Moses and exodus!
... Neil Armstrong and take the first step!
... Nixon and quit!
... an old man and retire!
... a soldier and march!
... a surgeon and cut out!

EXCRETION
Make like dandruff and flake off!
... diarrhea and run!
... a fart and blow away!
... horseshit and hit the trail!

CREATURE
Make like a ghost and fade away!
... a vampire and suck off!

ANIMAL
Make like an alligator and drag ass!
... an amoeba and split!
... an ant and crawl away!
... a bee and buzz off!
... a bird and fly away!
... a bird and leave the nest!
... a cow and moo(ve) it!
... a dodo bird and become extinct!
... a magician's rabbit and disappear!

PLANT
Make like a banana and peel!
... a banana and split!
... a date and dry up!
... a tree and embark!
... a tree and leave! [leaf]

OBJECT

Make like an Alka-Seltzer and dissolve!
    ... an aspirin and flake away!
    ... a candle and go out!
    ... a drum and beat it!
    ... a dryer and spin away!
    ... an egg and beat it!
    ... a fishing rod and cast off!
    ... an ice cube and melt away!
    ... a laxative and move out!
    ... a license and expire!
    ... a shoe and walk on!
    ... sugar and dissolve!
    ... a top and spin off!

VEHICLE

Make like an airplane and take off!
    ... a boat (ship) and shove off!
    ... a rocket and blast (lift) off!
    ... a ship and sail!

SOUND

Make like a rip and split!

ABSTRACT

Make like a bad sentence and run on!
    ... a mistake and exit!
    ... posterity and go back to the womb!
    ... war and evacuate!
    ... the wind and blow!

MISCELLANEOUS

Make like New York and light out!

There are some related simil-imperatives which perhaps should be included in this canon. "See you around like a toilet seat!", "See you around like a donut!" and "See you around if I don't see you square!"

The existence of these insulting simil-imperatives suggests a youthful reflection of the insulting humor of recent years practiced by Don Rickles, Rip Torn, and Johnny Carson. Is this, though, merely a nonce phenomenon like the "little moron" jokes of the 1940s and the "knock-knock" jokes of the 1950s? Perhaps they are indeed just a passing fad of the 1970s. If so, they should be recorded and preserved as folklore.

REFERENCES

Alexander, Bob. "Male and Female Rest Room Graffiti." *Maledicta* II (1978), 42-59.

Bronner, Simon J. "'Who says?': A Further Investigation of Ritual Insults Among White American Adolescents." *Midwestern Journal of Language and Folklore* IV, No. 2 (Fall, 1978), 53-69.

McCosh, Sandra. "Aggression in Children's Jokes." *Maledicta* I (1977), 125-32.

A Recipe for the Festive Season
TURKEY WITH POPCORN DRESSING
(Serves 12)

One 15-lb. Turkey
Seasonings
1 Can Bouillon
½ Cup Diced Celery

2 Cups Bread Crumbs
2 Diced Onions
3 Cups Popcorn

Method: Stuff turkey and bake at 325° about five hours, or until the popcorn blows the turkey's ass clear across the room.

Macabre Humor

Reinhold Aman

The latest Celebrity riddles—usually dealing with death or accidents of well-known personalities—were reported simultaneously from New Hampshire, Michigan and Wisconsin, in February 1984, and deal with Michael Jackson, the black singer whose hair caught on fire while filming a television commercial. Some of these jokes play on related accidents suffered by him and Richard Pryor, the black comedian whose body caught on fire while "freebasing" drugs. Several months before Jackson's accident, NBC newswoman Jessica Savitch drowned in her date's car in a canal; so far, I have received one "joke" about this tragedy. When actor Vic Morrow in 1982 was decapitated by helicopter blades during the filming of *Twilight Zone*, the Earl Mountbatten riddle (see 6:310) was reused. A couple of years ago, we had a rash of riddles about the deaths of Hollywood stars.

Such Celebrity jokes are particularly hard to take when "senseless" death is involved. The more bizarre the death, the more gruesome the jokes. There were jokes about Richard Speck, the Chicago nurse killer, and about various other mass murderers. The news (28 February 1984) about Robert Hansen, the Alaskan baker who admitted having raped 30 and killed at least 17 women, surely will result in some jokes and wordplays based on his profession, such as "How do you stop a baker from raping?" – "You twist his pecker into a pretzel."

To my knowledge, the biggest crop of macabre, black humor shot up after Edward Gein was arrested for multiple murders and other atrocities, recorded in the nightmare-inducing book *Edward Gein: America's Most Bizarre Murderer* (Delavan, Wis.: Chas. Hallberg & Co., 1981), brought to my attention by Pam, a Waukesha librarian. The following examples, from pages 211-212, make sense only if one knows the details: in 1957, Ed Gein, a 51-year-old hermit and bachelor, murdered several women, made a belt, wastepaper basket, lamp shades, chairs, bowls, and face masks of the victims' nipples, skulls, bones, and skin. He hung the corpses on meat hooks and eviscerated them like deer, cut off their heads, cut out their hearts, cut out their genitals and rectums (and wore them), ate and served to others their flesh, robbed graves, and was a necrophiliac. These revolting deeds shocked his Plainfield (pop. 642), Wisconsin, neighbors who tried to control their horror and reduce their fear by a wave of grim "Gein Humor" centering on cannibalism and sexual perversions. I have here recast in riddle form some of the clumsily-told examples:

What did Ed Gein say to his late-arriving guests?
— *"Sorry you weren't a little earlier. Everybody's eaten."*

What was Ed Gein's telephone number?
— *O-I-C-U-8-1-2.*

What did Ed Gein say when asked how his folks were?
— *"Delicious."*

Why couldn't Ed Gein operate his farm?
— *Because all he had left was a skeleton crew.*

What was the favorite beer in Plainfield?
— *Gein Beer: Lots of body but no head.*

What did Ed Gein say to the sheriff who arrested him?
— *"Have a heart."*

Why did they let Ed Gein out of the hospital on New Year's Eve?
— *So he could dig up a fresh date.*

How do you know that Ed Gein was really popular with girls?
— *Because there were always a lot of women hanging around his place.*

Why did Ed Gein's girl friend stop going with him?
— *Because he was such a cut-up.*

What did Ed Gein say when a hearse went by?
— *"Dig you later, Baby."*

What sign did Ed Gein have in his window?
— *"Wombs for Rent."*

Why did they have to keep the heat on in Ed Gein's house?
— *Because otherwise the furniture would get goose bumps.*

Why were there no mice around Ed Gein's farm house?
— *Because there were too many pussies.*

What article did Ed Gein write?
— *"I've Had My Fill of Women."*

Why wouldn't anyone play cards with Ed Gein?
— *Because he might come up with a good hand.*

Ethiopian Jokes

Richard Christopher

No serious student of American folk humor can fail to observe that the genre of "current event jokes" has become embedded with increasing depth and tenacity in the annals of verbal aggression. For more than two decades now, going back to the assassinations and watery embarrassment of the Brothers Kennedy, I have been collecting and recording such jokes; and, during the past five years, I have noted an astonishing increase in their range and sheer numbers.

Let a big story break—like those involving Billie Jean King, Karen Ann Quinlan, Renée Richards, Rosie Ruiz, Richard Pryor, Michael Jackson, Grace Kelly, Gerry Studds, Geraldine Ferraro, Jesse Jackson, Karen Carpenter, Natalie Wood, and Baby Fae, or the incidents at Big Dan's Pool Hall and the San Ysidro McDonald's—and within a week my far-reaching network of correspondents will have supplied me with one to ten quips about the event.

Reinhold Aman has added over two dozen new riddles to this collection, gathered from *Maledicta* readers and Henry Birdseye's computer bulletin board.

The story that most dominates our consciousness and consciences in 1985 has been the holocaust of famine and death that has devastated Ethiopia. As a member of the human race, I am staggered by the enormousness—and the enormity—of this vast tragedy. As a collector and recorder of verbal aggression, I note that this ultimate distillation of our most ghastly nightmares has spawned the greatest number of "current event jokes" that I have ever encountered.

What is an amateur scholar like me and a professional

journal like *Maledicta* to do with such information? First, we may speculate on the reasons why such a horror of an event would produce such a spate of jokes. Could the reason be the vastness of problem? The helplessness of the victims? The length of time the story has dominated the news? The sense of our own vulnerability in the face of the nuclear threat and the ecological fragility of the planet we all ride? Or could the reason be that black people are the ones who are doing the starving and dying?

Second, *Maledicta* and I can print the jokes. While we echo Kurtz's hollow cry in Joseph Conrad's *Heart of Darkness*—"The horror! The horror!"—we must also record the deeply human response to that horror in the form of the many Ethiopian jokes that have become a significant part of our current oral folklore. Here they are—all brief, all centering on starvation. Make of them what you will.

The earliest of the Ethiopian jokes was:

What's the fastest-moving flightless bird?
— *A chicken running through Ethiopia.* (Or *The Ethiopian chicken.*)

Why did the chicken cross the road?
— *He saw an Ethiopian coming after him.*

What's the lowest-selling product in Ethiopia?
— *After-dinner mints.* (Or *Maalox, laxatives, dental floss, table cloths, napkins, silverware, Tums,* etc.)

How many Ethiopians can you stuff into a phone booth?
— *All of them.*

How many Ethiopians can you fit into a shopping cart?
— *None. They fall through the holes.*

How many Ethiopians can you fit in a bathtub?
— *None. They keep sliding down the drain.*

What's black, round and covered with cobwebs?
— *An Ethiopian's asshole.*

What do you call an Ethiopian walking his dog?
— *A vegetarian.*

What do you call an Ethiopian walking two dogs?
— *A caterer.*

What do you call an Ethiopian walking ten dogs?
— *A rancher.*

What do you call an Ethiopian with long, stringy hair?
— *A mop.*

What do you call an Ethiopian wearing a turban (*or* Afro)?
— *A Q-Tip.*

What do you call an Ethiopian wearing a fur coat?
— *A pipe cleaner.*

What do you call an Ethiopian with a dime on his head?
— *A nail.*

What do you call an Ethiopian with a big toe?
— *A golf club.*

What do you call an Ethiopian with a swollen foot?
— *A three wood.*

What do you call an Ethiopian with a blue spot on his head?
— *A pool stick.*

What do you call an Ethiopian with a feather sticking out of his ass?
— *A dart.*

What do you call an Ethiopian with buck teeth?
— *A rake.*

What do you call an Ethiopian around a guy's neck?
— *Ty.*

What do you call an Ethiopian with a sesame seed bun on his head?
— *A quarter-pounder.*

What do you call a forty-pound Ethiopian?
— *"Bubba" or "Fatty."*

What's new about the McDonald's restaurant in Ethiopia?
— *It features a crawl-up window.*

What has millions of legs and weighs a thousand pounds?
— *The entire population of Ethiopia.*

Why don't Ethiopians go to movie theaters?
— *Because they can't keep the seats down.*

Who has body measurements of 18-38-18 (*or* 10-10-10)?
— *Miss Liberated Free People's Democratic Republic of Ethiopia.*

What do you call 125 Ethiopians in a Mercedes?
— *Brown corduroy slipcovers.*

What's a definition of "optimist"?
— *An Ethiopian wearing a dinner jacket.*

What is the Ethiopian national anthem?
— *"Aren't you hungry for a Burger King now?"*

What did Poland send to Ethiopia for famine relief?
— *4,000 pounds of after-dinner mints.*

What do Yoko Ono and Ethiopians have in common?
— *They both live off dead beetles.*

What does an Ethiopian use for a belt?
— *A rubber band.*

What do Ethiopians use key rings for?
— *Belts.*

How can you tell the Jewish Ethiopian?
— *He's the one wearing the fancy gold watch around his waist.*

Who's the patron saint of Ethiopia?
— *Karen Carpenter.*

What's the difference between an Ethiopian baby and an NFL football?
— *The football weighs at least 14 ounces.*

What's the difference between an Ethiopian and Levi's?
— *Levi's have only one fly.*

What does an Ethiopian do with a bag of potato chips?
— *He opens a restaurant.*

What's the nicest thing to say to an Ethiopian?
— *"My, you've gained weight lately."*

What's the meanest thing to say to an Ethiopian?
— *"What's for dinner?"*

How do you start a fire?
— *Rub two Ethiopians together.*

What does an Ethiopian feel after breakfast?
— *Guilt.*

What's the main cause of child disappearance in Ethiopia?
— *Breeze.*

What did the Ethiopian do when he fell into the alligator pit?
— *That sucker ate two before they could pull him out.*

How can you tell the sex of an unborn Ethiopian baby?
— *Hold the pregnant woman up to the light.*

What's the best thing about an Ethiopian blowjob?
— *You* know *she's going to swallow it.*

There are also visual jokes:

What's this? [With your index finger trace the fluttering path of a falling leaf.]
— *An Ethiopian jumping out of a tree.*

What's this? [Hold a fine-tooth comb vertically.]
— *Ethiopian bunk beds.*

What's this? [Hold a fine-tooth comb with the teeth facing up.]
— *Fifty Ethiopians in a canoe.*

What's this? [Pinch your neck on both sides of your Adam's apple and pull out.]
— *An Ethiopian with a grain of rice stuck in his throat.*

What is this? [Make a circle with your forefinger and thumb.]
— *An Ethiopian stranglehold.*

Aids Jokes

While collecting material on the Acquired Immune Deficiency Syndrome (AIDS), I came across several jokes and near-jokes. As with all humor, the purpose of these jokes is "to absorb and control, even slough off, by means of jocular presentation and laughter, the great anxiety that both teller and listener feel in connection with certain culturally determined themes."*

Legman, in his monumental tome on the dirty joke, correctly observes that puns and riddles are the simplest forms of joke. It is understandable that in a series of jokes precipitated by a particular—and recent—event such as AIDS, this should be the first and most frequent type of joke to be encountered.

— Casper G. Schmidt

What does GAY mean?
— *Got Aids Yet?*

What does AIDS stand for?
— *Ailment Indigenous to Dick Suckers.*

What does AIDS stand for?
— *Assholes In Deep Shit.*

What does AIDS stand for?
— *Anally Inserted Death Sentence.*

What's the most difficult thing an AIDS victim has to do?
— *Convince his parents that he's a Haitian.*

What do you call gays on roller skates?
— *ROLLAIDS.*

What club did the victims of AIDS found?
— *The 4-H Club:* Homos, Hemos, Haitians, Heroin addicts.

How does Anita Bryant spell relief?
— *A-I-D-S.*

Why are medical researchers having such trouble finding a cure for AIDS?
— *Because they're having a hell of a time teaching the lab mice how to butt-fuck.*

What do you call a group of gay musicians?
— *Band-AIDS.*

What do you call gay guys who run a projector?
— *Visual AIDS.*

How do gays spell relief?
— *N-O-A-I-D-S.*

What's the difference between herpes and AIDS?
— *Herpes is a love story, and AIDS is a fairy tale.*

What's the new name for AIDS?
— *Toxic Cock Syndrome.*

What do you call a faggot without AIDS?
— *One lucky cocksucker.*

What did they name the new AIDS hospital between Dallas and Fort Worth?
— *"Sick Fags Over Texas."*

What's the great mystery about AIDS?
— *It can turn a fruit into a vegetable.*

* Gershon Legman (1968), *Rationale of the Dirty Joke: An Analysis of Sexual Humor.* Castle Books, pp. 13-14.

Miscellany

♦ Ambrose Bierce's *Enlarged Devil's Dictionary*, ed. by Ernest Hopkins (1967), describes the common housefly as **musca maledicta**, "damned, cursèd fly." (Robert Smith)

♦ "**My sharp Cheddar Balls are back....**" (Advertisement in *The Adventurous Cheeselover: International Cheese Newsletter*, N.Y., March 1981, p. 4. — Thanks for telling us, Gerard)

♦ Found in "Dr. Wing Tip Shoo's X-Rated Fortune Cookies" (N.Y.): **Woman who cooks carrots and peas in same pot, unsanitary. — Stenographer not permanent fixture until screwed on desk. — Girl who sleep with judge get honorable discharge.** (Page Bernstein)

♦ *Q:* What's the difference between a vitamin and a hormone? *A:* You can make a vitamin. ("Benny Hill Show")

♦ John Lahr published the biography of Joe Orton (1978) called **Prick Up Your Ears**. (Rather messy, and painful.)

♦ Does your female sexual partner treat you like your banker? "**Substantial penalties for early withdrawal.**"

♦ **Happiness is a Good Screw.** (Advertising on matchbox cover, Tyco Fastening Products, N.Y. — Keith Denning)

♦ *Poetic Justice:* When your brother-in-law who neither smokes, drinks nor swears catches VD. (Roy West)

♦ **Garden Bouquet** Beauty Soap: New brand name for the former **Gay Bouquet** soap. (Henry Madden)

♦ Would you say that a seven-year-old homosexual is a kid who turned prematurely gay?

♦ The headquarters of **Women USA** (Bella Abzug, president) is located in N.Y. City, **76 Beaver St.** (Denison Hatch)

♦ Baltimore Police Commissioner Donald Pomerleau, testifying in a sex discrimination lawsuit: "All women are little balls of fluff in the eyes of the creator." (*Debris* 8, June 1981, p. 2. — John Boston). The Creator must have been blind in the case of Abzug, Friedan & Co.: nothing fluffy about them!

♦ After Tennis Star Billie Jean King's lesbian affair became known, jokes started to fly: *Q:* Who will be B.J.K.'s new sponsor? *A:* Snap-on Tools. — *Q:* How did Billie become champion? *A:* She licked her opponents. — *Q:* Why won't they let Billie play at the World Championship in Holland? *A:* Because she wants to stick her finger in every dike. (Dennis D., Gordon W.)

Maledicta Contributors

REINHOLD AMAN, Ph.D., is the editor and publisher of *Maledicta*.

LEONARD R.N. ASHLEY, Ph.D., is Professor of English at Brooklyn College of The City University of New York.

GIULIANO AVERNA is a poet, novelist, and translator whose works appear in magazines and anthologies.

SCOTT BEACH is an actor, broadcaster, and author. A Fulbright scholar, he has studied at the Sorbonne and the Conservatoire National de Musique in France.

BOB BURTON BROWN is Professor of Education at the University of Florida and a former Dean of the University College. His publishing credits include *Common Scents: The First Book of Farts*.

*RICHARD CHRISTOPHER holds a Ph.D. in English.

MARTHA CORNOG holds an M.A. in Linguistics and Masters of Library Science. She is a consultant, technical writer, and editor.

DAN CRAGG honorably concluded 22 years of active military service and retired as a Sergeant Major. He is one of the leading experts on the life of 18th-century satirist Francis Grose.

BRIGITTA GELTRICH-LUDGATE is a Faculty and Staff Trainer at the Defense Language Institute in Monterey, California.

*L. HERRERA is a full-time professional translator of technical and commercial documents, with an interest in cross-cultural communication.

WESTON LA BARRE, James B. Duke Professor of Anthropology Emeritus, has authored many books and articles.

G. LEGMAN is the world's leading authority of erotic folklore and literature. He has been the official bibliographer for the Kinsey Institute. His book, *No Laughing Matter*, won First Prize in the University of Chicago's Folklore competition in 1976.

DOUGLAS LINDSEY, M.D., is a surgeon at the University of Arizona in Tucson, and has devoted 30 years of service to the U.S. Army Medical Corps.

LOIS MONTEIRO is Associate Professor of Medical Sciences at Brown University, Rhode Island.

STEPHEN O. MURRAY, Ph.D., is Research Associate at the Language Behavior Research Laboratory at the University of California, Berkeley.

DON L.F. NILSEN, Ph.D., has written several scholarly books on language and is Director of Linguistics at Arizona State University.

FRANK H. NUESSEL, Ph.D., is Associate Professor of Spanish and Director of the Program in Linguistics at the University of Louisville.

JOSEPH S. SALEMI teaches English at Pace University and Marymount Manhattan College in New York City.

C.J. SCHEINER is a surgeon in New York and a collector of erotica and curiosa.

CASPER G. SCHMIDT, M.D., is Associate Director of the Institute for Psychohistory and has a private practice as a child psychiatrist in New York.

ROBERT M. SCHUMACHER studied at Eastern Illinois University, majoring in speech communication and psychology.

LAURENCE E. SEITS is Professor of English at Waubonsee Community College in Illinois. He has a scholarly interest in names.

ANDREW R. SISSON teaches French at Phillips Exeter Academy in Exeter, New Hampshire. He holds degrees from Harvard, the University of Notre Dame, and the University of Geneva.

JOHN SOLT is a doctoral candidate in East Asian Languages at Harvard University and presently teaches English in Japan.

MARIO E. TERUGGI is a linguist, literary critic, and novelist. He is Senior Professor in the School of Natural Sciences and Museum of La Plata University in Argentina.

*Pseudonym.

Index

Academic graffiti, 75–76, 77–89
AIDS jokes, 194–195
Arab joke, 144
Asians. *See* Orientals
Authority figures, jokes about, 70–72

Bawdy jokes, 26–28
Birth control graffiti, 81–82
Blacks
   jokes about, 103–106, 141, 142, 144, 145, 146, 148
   ritual insults, 120, 121–124, 131–134
   verbal contests, 15
Blasphemies, 40–47
Blindness, jokes about, 142, 146, 148
Bodily parts, 13, 108–115
   See also Names of body parts

Breaking wind, 19–25
British slang, 29–34, 37

Cannibalism, 187–188
Canting, 29
Carter, Jimmy, 107
Celebrities, jokes about, 141, 142, 146, 185–187
Charles, Ray, 148
Charles and Diana joke, 145
Chastity, 17–18
Child molestation joke, 142
Children's jokes and riddles, 61–74
Chinese jokes, 147
Christ
   jokes about, 147
   references to, 40, 43, 45
Colorful language, 9–18
Compliments, rough, 11
Computer and offensive language, 93

Davis, Sammy, Jr., 146, 148
Derek, Bo, 148
Devaluation, 129–130
Dishonesty, 14

Ethiopian jokes, 188–193
Ethnic jokes, 72, 100. *See also specific groups*
Exvitations, 180–184

Falwell, Jerry, 147
Family insults, 15
Farting
   euphemisms for, 19–24
   jokes about, 145
   styles of, 25
Feminist movement, 82–83
Fetishes, 83
Folk speech, 9–18
Foreign phrase books, 55–60
French
   jokes about, 146, 148
   sexual language, 92
   slang, 35–37

Gay. *See* Homosexuals; Lesbian
Gein, Edward, 186–187
Genitals. *See also* Penis; Vulva
   pet names for, 108–117
Genitomorphism, 113–114
German jokes, 145, 147
God
   graffiti about, 75
   references to, 16, 40–41, 43–47
Graffiti
   academic, 75–76, 77–89
   dialogue, 78, 90
   sexual, 77–89, 90
Greek joke, 145

Hair, 83–84
Haitian joke, 144
Hansen, Robert, 186
Hillbillies, 141
Homosexual imagery, 16
Homosexual insults, 75, 85–86, 123, 135
   ritual, 124–130, 132–135
Homosexuals, jokes about, 140, 141, 142, 143, 144, 145, 146, 147, 194–195, 196
Humor. *See also* Jokes; Riddles
   insulting, 180–184

macabre, 185–187

Illegitimacy, 10
Incest
   graffiti about, 86–87
   mother–son, 10
Indians, jokes about, 148
Insults
   all-purpose, 10–17
   black, 120, 121–124
      ritual, 131–134
   English vocabulary, 36
   homosexual ritual, 132–135
   of homosexuals, 123, 124–130
   Italian, 40–41
   Japanese, 48–54
   medical, 170–173, 174–179
      specialities, 178
   to mothers, 121–122, 124
   to nurses, 175
   ornithological, 162–169
   playing, 118–119, 131–135
   ritual in stigmatized subcultures, 118–140
   sexual, 48–54, 122, 125–128
   Spanish, 38–39
   used by teenagers, 180–184
   of women, 17–18, 121–122, 124
Intelligence, insults to, 12–13
Iranians, jokes about, 148
Italian blasphemies, 40–41, 42–47
Italian jokes, 142, 145

Jackson, Michael, 185–186
Japanese sexual insults, 48–54
Jewish American Princess, jokes about, 147
Jewish mothers, jokes about, 147
Jewish ritual insults, 131
Jews, jokes about, 141, 144, 145, 146, 147
Jokes, 61–74. *See also* names of *individuals;* names of *groups of persons*
   in academic graffiti, 75–76

about AIDS, 194–195
against oneself, 69–72
against peers, 67–69
bawdy, 26–28
celebrity, 141, 142, 146, 185–187
current events, 188
dirty, 65, 114
insulting, 180–184. *See also* Insults, ritual
political, 107
racial, 103–106
scatological, 69, 142
sexual, 67–68, 196
about starvation, 188–193

Keller, Helen, 142, 146
King, Billie Jean, 196

Lesbian jokes, 143, 144, 196
License plate taboos, 98–102
Love graffiti, 88–89

Macabre humor, 185–187
Macho imagery, 16–17
Madonna, references to, 40–41, 43, 47
Marriage graffiti, 81
Masturbation, 11, 49, 91–92, 93
Medical insults, 170–179
Medical slang, 170–173, 174–179
Morrow, Vic, 186
Mother, 147
  insults to, 121–122, 124
  references to, 39–39
Mountbatten, Earl, 186

Nixon, Richard, 81, 84
Norms, jokes about, 72
Nuns, jokes about, 147
Nurses, insults of, 175

Obscene language. *See also* Profanity
  on computers, 93
  in riddles, 65
Onassis, Jackie, 148
Oral sex, 87–88
Orgasm
  female, 96–97
  male, 95–96
Orientals, jokes about, 146

Ornithological insults, 162–169
Pejoratives. *See* Insults
Penis, pet names for, 109–110
Personal shortcomings, 69–70
Polish jokes, 142, 144, 146, 148
Political jokes, 107
Poonerisms, 26–28
Premature ejaculation, 94–95
Priests
  joke about, 146
  references to, 45
Profanity, 8–18, 40–47. *See also* Obscene language
Prostitutes
  graffiti about, 87
  joke about, 147
Pryor, Richard, 185–186
Puerto Rican jokes, 142

Racial slurs/insults, 103–106
Rape, 87
Reagan, Nancy, 141
Reagan, Ronald, 107
Religious jokes, 143–144, 147
Religious profanity, 40–41, 42–47
Religious taboos in license plates, 101
Riddles, 61–74
  celebrity, 185–187
  thinking, 63
Ridicule
  of peers, 67–69
  of self, 69–72

Santa Claus joke, 148
Savitch, Jessica, 186
Scatological humor, 28, 69, 142
Scatological images, 11–13
  in license plates, 100
School, jokes about, 71–72
Schwarzenegger, Arnold, 145
Sex discrimination, 196
Sexist language, 94–97
Sexist slang, 35–37
Sexual graffiti, 77–89
Sexual imagery, 17–18
Sexual insults, 41
  Japanese, 48–54
Sexual jokes, 67–68, 143, 144, 145, 146, 148, 196

Sexual language
  by computer users, 93
  double entendres, 55–60, 107
  for genitals, 108–114
  in license plates, 101–102
  for sexual intercourse, 94–97
  Yugoslavian, 55–60
Sexual perversion, 187
Sexual slang, 29–34, 35–37
Sickness. *See* Insults, medical; Medical slang
Signifying, 15
Simil-imperatives, 180–184
Slang
  British, 37
  Cockney rhyming, 29–34
  expressions, 9–18
  medical, 170–173, 174–179
  sexual, 29–34, 35–37
  of youth, 35–37
Sounding, 15
Spanish insults, 38–39
Speck, Richard, 186
Spoonerisms in bawdy jokes, 26–28
Swinging, 87

Taboo terms, 65–66, 68, 98–102
  anatomical, 99–100
Taylor, Elizabeth, 146
Teachers, jokes about, 71
Teenage jokes and riddles, 61–74

Ugliness, 14

Veneral disease, 84, 196
Verbal aggression, 180–184
Verbal contests, 14–15
Vietnam experience, 149–161
Viet-Speak, 149–161
Violence, language of, 149–161
Vulva, pet names for, 110–114

Welfare jokes, 147
Women
  insults of, 17–18
  jokes about, 141, 142, 143, 196
Word play, 78–79

Yugoslavia, 55–60